D

Earth-Friendly OUTDOOR FUN

The Earth-Friendly Series

Earth-Friendly Toys

How to Make Fabulous Toys and Games
from Reusable Objects

Earth-Friendly Wearables

How to Make Fabulous Clothes and Accessories
from Reusable Objects

Earth-Friendly Holidays

How to Make Fabulous Gifts and Decorations
from Reusable Objects

Earth-Friendly Outdoor Fun

How to Make Fabulous Games, Gardens, and
Other Projects from Reusable Objects

Earth-Friendly OUTDOOR FUN

How to Make Fabulous Games, Gardens, and Other Projects from Reusable Objects

George Pfiffner

John Wiley & Sons, Inc.

New York • Chichester • Brisbane • Toronto • Singapore

Copyright © 1996 by Tenth Avenue Editions, Inc.
Published by John Wiley & Sons, Inc.
All rights reserved. Published simultaneously in Canada.

The publisher and the author have made every reasonable effort to ensure that the experiments and activities in this book are safe when conducted as instructed but assume no responsibility for any damage caused or sustained while performing the experiments or activities in the book. Parents, guardians, and/or teachers should supervise young readers who undertake the experiments and activities in this book.

Library of Congress Cataloging-in-Publication Data

Pfiffner, George
    Earth-friendly outdoor fun : how to make fabulous games, gardens, and other projects from reusable objects / George Pfiffner.
        p.   cm.– (The Earth-friendly series)
    Summary: Includes step-by-step instructions on how to convert materials such as scrap cardboard and plastic bottles into items for outdoor fun and use.
        ISBN 0-471-14113-5 (paper : alk. paper)
        1. Dress accesories–Juvenile literature. 2. Handicraft–Juvenile literature. 3. Recycling (Waste, etc.)–Juvenile literature. [1. Handicraft. 2. Recycling (Waste)]   I. Title. II. Series.
    TT560.P43   1996
    745.5–dc20   95-51773

Produced for John Wiley & Sons, Inc.
by Tenth Avenue Editions, Inc.
Creative Director: Clive Giboire
Assistant Editor: Matthew Moore
Editorial Assistants: Suzanne Cobban, Judy Myers, Victoria Russell
Artist: George Pfiffner
Photographs: George Roos

Printed in the United States of America

10 9 8 7 6 5 4 3 2 1

Foreword

Every day when we open our mail at the Environmental Action Coalition, we find letters from young people all over the country. We have probably received a letter from your town, maybe even from your school.

Sometimes the letters ask questions, such as "How can we start a recycling program?" or "How does a landfill work?"

Sometimes they report on recycling projects kids have started, such as "We use both sides of our notebook paper" and "Our Boy Scout troop collected 392,000 cans."

We are always glad to get letters like these because we have been working on recycling since 1970, when only a few people were involved. Today people are coming up with more and more ideas about recycling.

Young people have made a big difference. You have come up with new ideas. Many of you have started recycling programs in your schools. You have taught your parents and grandparents how important recycling is, so the whole family can help keep the environment clean.

This is a very important moment in the history of the environmental movement. Young people all over the world are working together to try to save our planet from being buried under garbage.

As you can see from the globe on the cover of this book, you are part of an international movement. We all have a lot to learn from each other.

Have you heard the slogan **Reduce, Reuse, and Recycle**? These three simple words will give you the key to taking environmental action.

Reduce the amount of garbage you create. This means telling the person in the store that you don't need a bag to carry what you bought.

Reuse means finding a new life for something instead of throwing it away. That's what this book is all about.

Recycle means taking used materials and making them into materials that can be used again—like turning old newspaper into newspaper that can be printed on again.

Whether you are already an active recycler or are just getting started, this new series of books will give you many projects that you and your friends can make using things that would otherwise be thrown away.

If you enjoy the projects in this book, the next step is to show your friends how to make them.

You might also come up with some of your own ideas for projects. If you do, I'm sure the publisher would like to hear about them, so write them down. Who knows, maybe they'll be in the next book.

If you like the idea of recycling stuff, then you can look into what kind of recycling program your community has, or you can start a recycling program in your school. Ask your teacher for help.

But now it's time to get out your scissors and pencils and paste so you can get to work. Have a great time!

Steve Richardson
Executive Director
Environmental Action Coalition

Contents

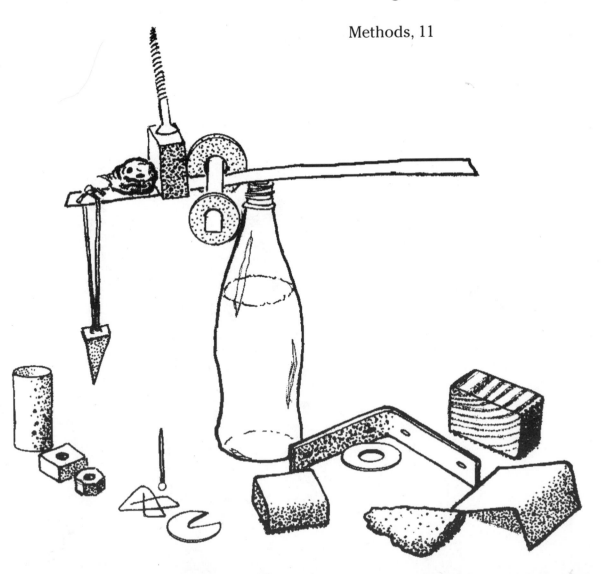

GARDENING

OTHER OUTDOOR FUN

WEATHER FUN

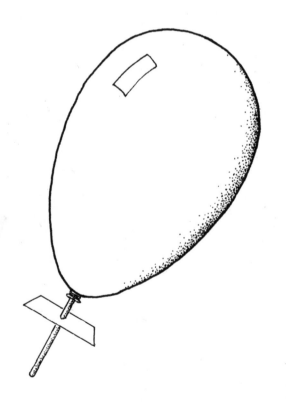

Being Earth-Friendly

Across the country and around the world, people are learning to reduce, reuse, and recycle. We have only one Earth, so we need to learn how to take care of it. We need to learn how to be "Earth-Friendly."

Some people think that recycling is just about washing out cans and tying up newspapers. But we think that recycling is really about rethinking—seeing the things around you in a new way.

When you start thinking about things in a new way, you can see that what used to be a jar is now a barometer, and what used to be a soda bottle is now a bowling pin. This book, and the other books in this series, are about using your imagination to make new things out of old "trash."

In this book, there are 25 outdoor projects for you to make. Every project is made out of already used materials. As you learn how to make cool outdoor projects, you will also be learning how to help the environment. We've included information about recycling and tips on how you can help.

But the most important thing about this book is that it's fun! Every project in this book is fun to do. Even when you've made all the outdoor projects in the book, the skills and ideas are yours forever. Who knows where your imagination will lead you.

Getting Started

Making your projects will be much easier if you follow all the instructions carefully. Here are some tips to get you started.

Before You Do Anything
Read all the instructions and look at the drawings **before** you start making a project. The more you know about how the project is made, the easier it will be to follow the steps.

Level of Difficulty
Each project is rated according to how easy it is to complete. Here's a key to the symbols used to rate each project:

 = quick and easy

 = little time and medium difficulty

 = time-consuming and challenging

You might want to start with some of the easier and faster projects until you get the hang of following the instructions.

Work Time
Set aside plenty of time to work on each project, and give it your full attention. Your outdoors projects will turn out better if you don't hurry and if you aren't distracted.

Workplace
After choosing a project to make, decide on the best place to work. Some projects require more space than others. For example, The Scarecrow needs a big work surface.

Materials
Before you start, get together everything you will need for the project. Put all the tools and materials on or near your work surface so that you can find them easily while you are working.

Some materials are easy to find at home. For some projects you will have to collect the materials you need from outside your home. Don't be discouraged if you don't have exactly the materials we suggest. In many of the projects you can substitute materials. Ask an **adult helper** to help you decide if a substitute will work.

Recycling Facts and Tips
Some projects have Recycling Facts and Tips at the end. These are ideas about how you can rethink and recycle every day.

Symbols You Will Need to Know

! Steps marked with an **!** need to be done with an **adult helper**. If you don't have an **adult** to help you, don't try this project.

✪ **Even Better:** This indicates ideas about how to make your outdoor projects more interesting.

Have Fun!

Methods

The methods on the next few pages are shortcuts that are used in many of the projects. You may want to try them out before you start working on your first outdoor project.

The Pushpin Method is useful when you need to cut heavy material or when you need to cut "windows."

The Transfer Method will make it easy to transfer patterns from the book to paper, cardboard, or cloth.

The Center-Finding Method will help you find the exact center of any circle.

The Whip-Stitch Method will help you join the edges of two pieces of fabric.

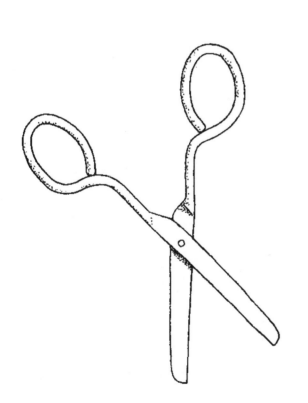

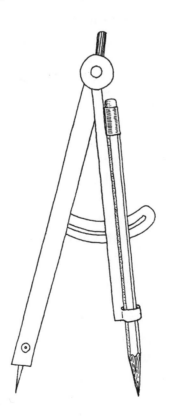

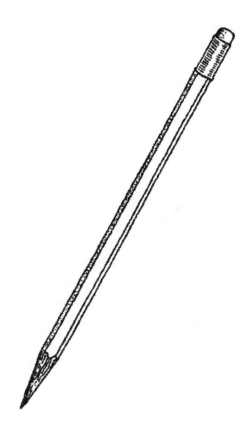

The Pushpin Method

*This method is useful when you need to cut
heavy material or when you need to cut "windows."*

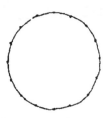

Punch holes at even intervals around
the shape you want to cut.

You Need

- ❏ a pencil
- ❏ a pushpin
- ❏ scissors

Instructions

1. Draw the line or shape to be cut.

2. Punch holes along the line or shape with the pushpin.

3. If the material you're cutting is **light** (such as light cardboard or thin plastic), you only need to make a few pushpin holes to start and guide the cut. Then use scissors to finish cutting.

4. If the material you're cutting is **heavy** and would be difficult to cut with scissors (such as heavy cardboard or thick plastic), you can make the entire cut with the pushpin alone.

    a. Make pushpin holes at even intervals on the cut line, as shown.

    b. Now make holes between those holes.

    c. Then make a third series of holes between the holes you've already punched.

    d. Once you've punched a lot of holes close together, you should be able to pull the pieces apart or push the shape out.

5. If you need to cut a square or rectangle, first mark each corner with a pushpin hole. Then make your other pushpin holes working from corner to corner.

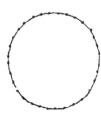

Then punch holes between those holes.

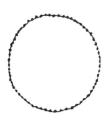

Then punch a third set of holes between **those** holes.

To cut right-angle corners, make pushpin holes along both edges.

The Transfer Method

For some of the projects in this book you will need to transfer patterns from the book to paper, cardboard, or cloth. This method will make that easy to do.

You Need

- ❏ tracing paper
- ❏ tape
- ❏ a soft pencil
- ❏ a pencil sharpener
- ❏ a hard pencil

Instructions

1. Working on a smooth, level surface, place the tracing paper over the design or pattern you want to transfer. Tape all four corners of the tracing paper to the pattern to keep the tracing paper from moving.

2. Trace the lines of the pattern onto the tracing paper using a soft pencil. Sharpen the pencil often so that the lines are clear and neat.

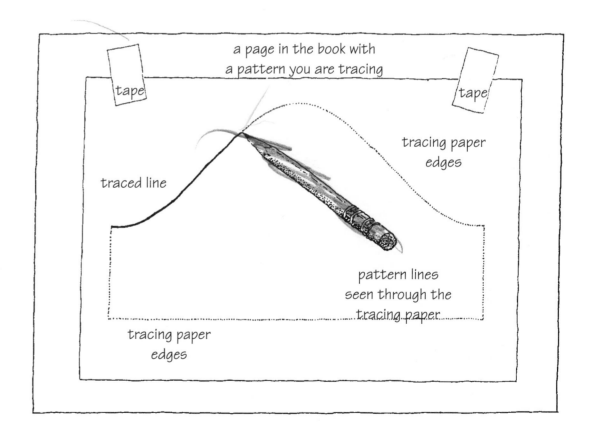

a page in the book with a pattern you are tracing

tape

tape

tracing paper edges

traced line

pattern lines seen through the tracing paper

tracing paper edges

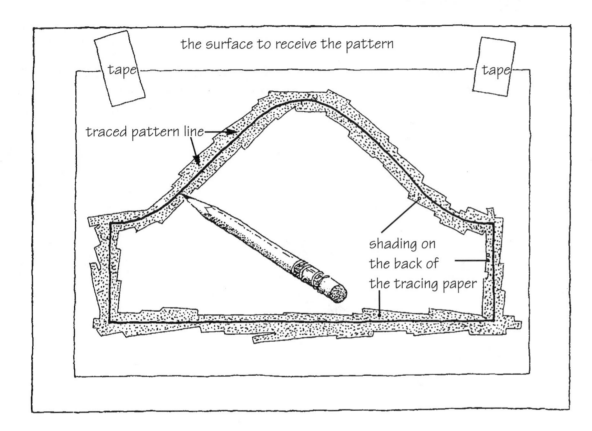

the surface to receive the pattern

tape

tape

traced pattern line

shading on
the back of
the tracing paper

5. Turn the tracing back over and tape it onto the surface you've selected for the pattern. Transfer the pattern to that surface by retracing over the lines, this time with the hard pencil. Be sure to go over each line carefully.

6. You can lift up a corner of the tracing paper to check that the pattern is being transferred clearly. If it isn't, add more shading with the soft pencil.

7. When the entire pattern has been transferred, you may want to darken the lines with a pencil.

3. When you have finished tracing the pattern, remove the tape and turn the tracing paper over.

4. Use a soft pencil to cover all the lines on the back side with pencil shading. Use the side of the pencil lead to make the shading.

The Center-Finding Method

Use this method to find the exact center of any circle.

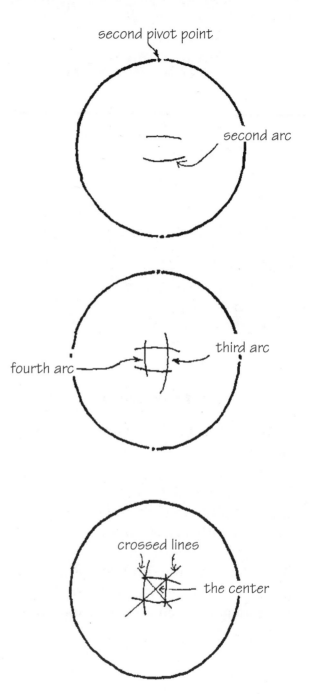

second pivot point

second arc

third arc

fourth arc

crossed lines

the center

You Need

- ❏ a compass (for drawing circles)
- ❏ a pencil
- ❏ a ruler

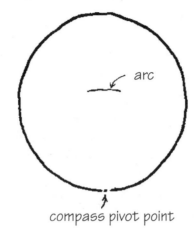

arc

compass pivot point

Instructions

1. Set your compass to a little more than half the diameter of the circle whose center you want to find. (The diameter is an imaginary line that goes from edge to edge through the center of a circle.)

2. Put the pivot (the pointed end) of the compass anywhere on the edge of the circle and draw a small arc (curved line) inside the circle.

3. Place the pivot of the compass on the circle across from the first point and draw a second small arc inside the circle.

4. Place the pivot on the circle one quarter of the way around from the second point and draw a third small arc inside the circle.

5. Now place the pivot on the circle directly across from the third point and draw a small arc inside the circle.

6. Use the ruler and pencil to draw two diagonal lines connecting the points where the four small arcs cross.

7. The point where the two lines cross is the exact center of the circle.

The Whip-Stitch Method

The whip stitch is used to join the edges of two pieces of fabric in a seam. You can also use the whip stitch to attach a patch to a piece of fabric.

You Need

❏ straight pins
❏ a threaded needle

Instructions

1. Make sure the thread has a knot in one end.

2. Line up the edges of the fabric so that they are even. Pin the edges together with straight pins.

3. Push the needle through both pieces of fabric near their edges. Pull the thread through the fabric until it is stopped by the knot.

4. Loop the thread over the edge, and push the needle up through the fabric again, about ¼ inch (.6 cm) away from the first stitch, making sure that the needle always comes through the cloth in the same direction.

5. Repeat along the length of the joined edges.

6. When you have sewn along the entire edge, tie a knot around the last stitch and cut the thread.

7. Remove the straight pins.

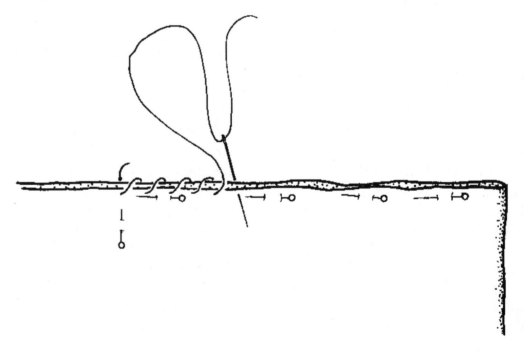

Outdoor Games

Bowling Game

Why go to the bowling alley when you can set up your very own bowling game in your backyard or basement? And it's a fun way to make use of all of those empty plastic soda bottles you probably have lying around.

You Need

- ❏ ten empty plastic soda bottles with caps, .5-liter size
- ❏ two old tennis balls

Have on Hand

- ❏ a pencil
- ❏ scrap paper
- ❏ water

Number of Players

- ❏ one to six

Instructions

To Make the Pins:

1. Rinse out the bottles and remove any labels.

2. Fill each bottle with water up to the rigid line near the bottom of the bottle. Try to put the same amount of water in each bottle. This will keep the bottles from falling over too easily.

Fill the bottle with water up to here.

To Play:

3. Find a level area to set up the bottles, such as a porch or basement floor. Do not set them up on the street.

4. Arrange the bottles in a triangle, as shown above, with four in the back row, three in the next row, two in the next row, and one in the front.

5. Use a stick, stone, or other object as a marker. Place the marker 10 feet (3 m) from the bottles.

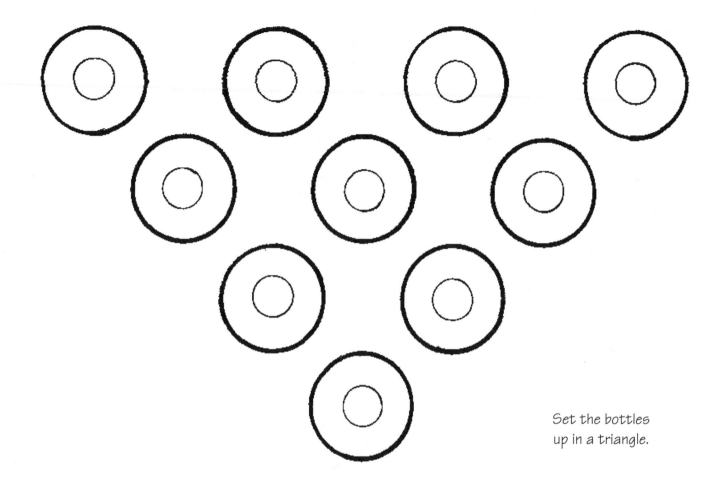

Set the bottles
up in a triangle.

6. Stand behind the marker and roll the balls one at a time at the bottles. How many bottles can you knock over with one ball?

7. Set the pins back up and invite some friends to play. Each player rolls one ball in a turn. Use a pencil and paper to keep score.

To Score:

8. If all the bottles are knocked over, the player gets 15 points.

9. If only some of the bottles are toppled, the number of bottles knocked over is the score. For example, if four bottles are knocked over, the score is 4.

10. Each player sets up the bottles for the next player.

11. Ten sets of turns make up one game. The player with the highest score at the end of the game wins.

King of the Hill Flag

Stake this earth-friendly flag on top of a hill and declare your recycled kingdom. But beware: anyone who can push you off the hill gets to be king!

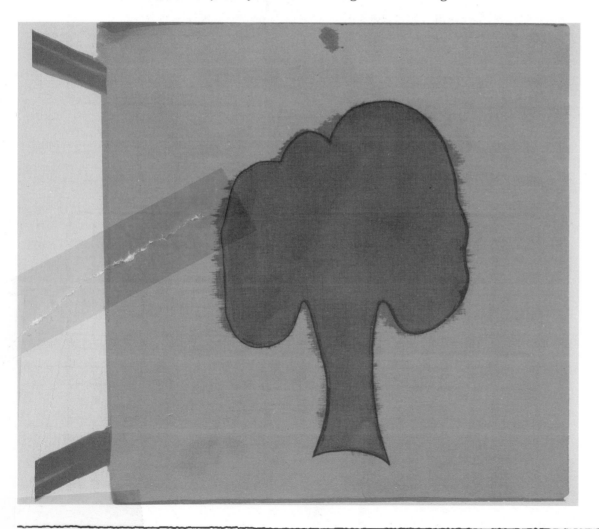

You Need

- ❏ a piece of old, white bed-sheet, 30 × 28 inches (75 × 70 cm)
- ❏ an old broom handle (or other tall, straight stick)

Have on Hand

- ❏ black and green marking pens
- ❏ heavy scrap paper, such as cut from a paper bag, 11 × 15 inches (27.5 × 37.5 cm)

Tools

- ❏ a pencil
- ❏ a ruler
- ❏ scissors

Number of Players

- ❏ as many as you like

Instructions

1. Fold the scrap paper in half lengthwise, then into quarters, and finally into eighths.

2. Repeat step **1**, this time folding the paper the other way, as shown.

3. Smooth out the paper.

4. Using the fold lines as guides, draw a grid on the bag with a pencil and ruler.

5. Enlarge the Tree Pattern (page 26) onto the brown paper by drawing each part of the pattern in the correct grid square. Don't worry if you make mistakes—it doesn't need to be perfect.

6. Cut out the paper tree with scissors.

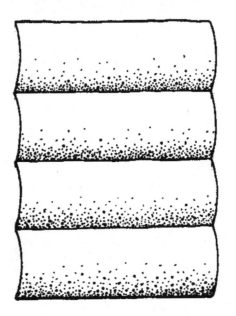
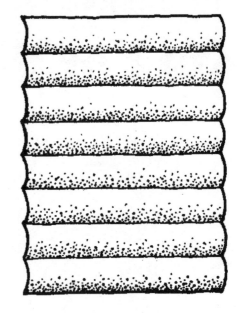
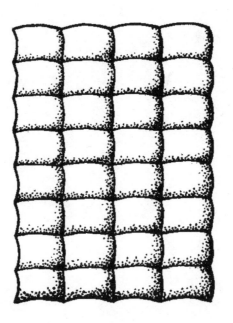
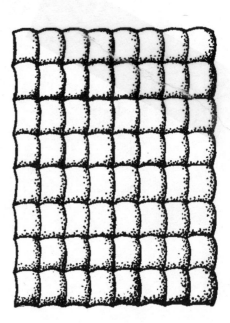

7. Use a marking pen and ruler to mark the dimensions of the flag onto the sheet. The measurements should be 30 inches (75 cm) wide by 28 inches (70 cm) high (refer to the diagram below).

8. Cut out the flag, making sure to leave extra material for ties at the top and bottom, as shown. The ties should be 10 inches (25 cm) long and about 4 inches (10 cm) wide.

9. Place the paper tree pattern on the flag. Draw around the outline of the pattern with a black marking pen.

10. Color in the tree with a green marking pen. When you are finished, turn the flag over and fill in any places where the color is weak.

11. Use the scissors to cut the flag ties in half lengthwise. Tie the flag ties around the broom handle tightly, so the flag doesn't slide down the handle.

12. Stake your flag anywhere as a symbol of being earth-friendly, or use it to play King of the Hill or Capture the Flag.

Rules for King of the Hill:

13. Stake your flag on the top of a hill or small mound.

14. The other players try to push you off the hill and claim your flag.

15. The person who can successfully defend the hill against all challengers wins.

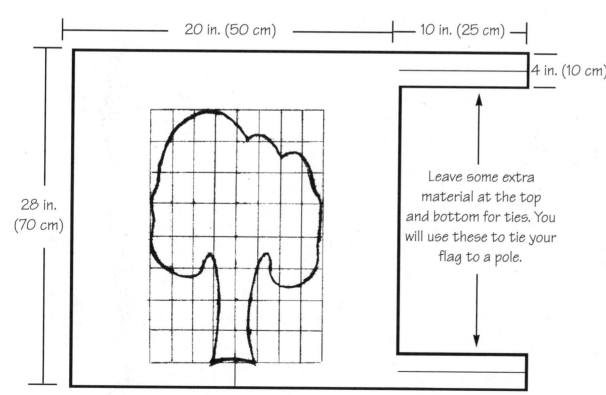

20 in. (50 cm) 10 in. (25 cm)

4 in. (10 cm)

28 in. (70 cm)

Leave some extra material at the top and bottom for ties. You will use these to tie your flag to a pole.

Tree Pattern

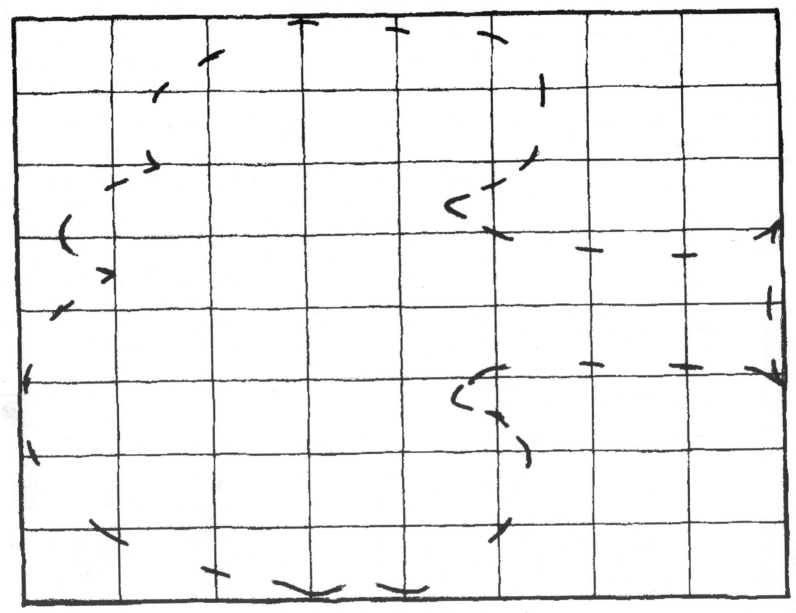

Copy the Tree Pattern onto the brown paper by
copying the lines in each grid square shown here
onto the same grid square on the paper.

Mini-Pinball Box

*This challenging game will provide hours
of fun alone or with a friend. It may seem easy,
but it's harder than it looks!*

You Need

❑ a small cardboard box
   (such as a matchbox or
   jewelry box)
❑ five BBs (or small,
   round beads)

Tools

❑ a large eraser
❑ a pencil
❑ a pushpin
❑ a ruler

Number of Players

❑ one or two

Instructions

1. Use the pencil and ruler to draw lines from corner to corner on the outside bottom of the box.

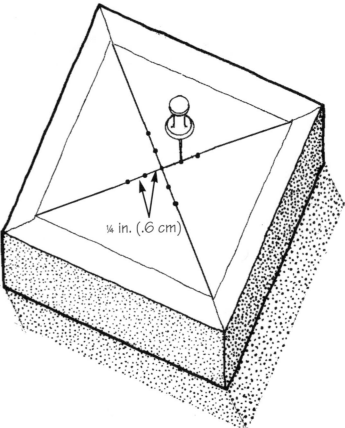

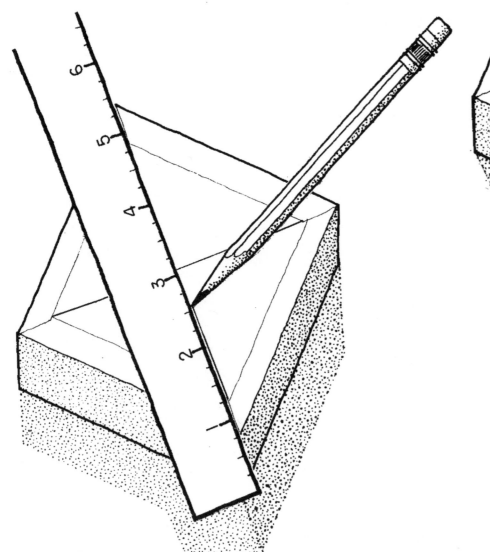

¼ in. (.6 cm)

2. Make two pencil marks on each line, ¼ inch (.6 cm) on each side of the point where the lines cross.

3. Make four more marks ¼ inch (.6 cm) out from the first four marks.

4. Use the pushpin to make small holes at each of the pencil marks.

5. From the inside of the box, enlarge each pushpin hole with the point of a sharpened pencil.

6. Each hole will have a slight ridge around it. Place the box on top of the eraser and press a BB down on each of the holes one by one to flatten the ridge and indent the holes slightly.

Note: Use the eraser end of a pencil to press down the BBs if it is too difficult to do with your fingers.

To Play:

7. Place five BBs loose in the box.

8. Tilt the box to roll the BBs into the holes in any regular pattern, such as all five BBs in a row.

9. If you want to compete with a friend, agree on a pattern that you will both try to get. Once a BB has fallen into a hole, you can't shake it out, but you can knock it out with other BBs.

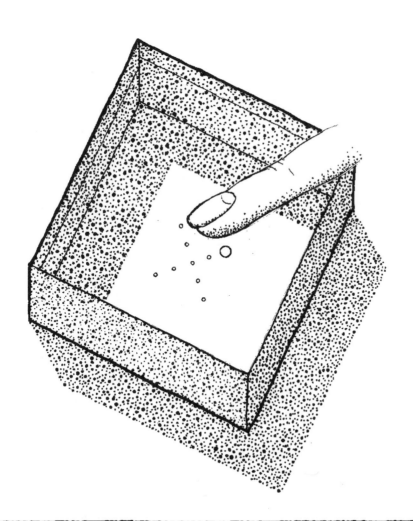

Penny Toss Game

Test your skill at this challenging game, made from a recycled egg carton. Then test your math skills by tallying up the score.

Instructions

1. Starting at one corner of the cardboard, use the ruler to measure 2 inches (5 cm) down the short end. Mark the spot with a pencil.

2. Use the scissors to make a cut 1¾ inches (4.4 cm) into the cardboard at the spot you have just marked.

3. Repeat steps **1** and **2** at the opposite end of the cardboard, as shown.

4. Use a pushpin to score (scratch a line along) the fold lines of the flaps you have just cut.

5. Fold the flaps inward, as shown.

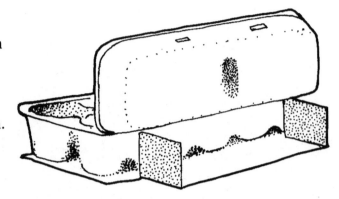

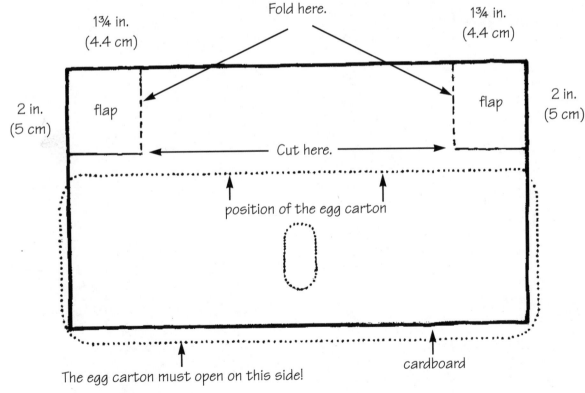

6. Spread stick glue on the bottom of the egg carton.

7. Place the egg carton on the cardboard, as shown. Press the carton firmly onto the cardboard so the glue sets.

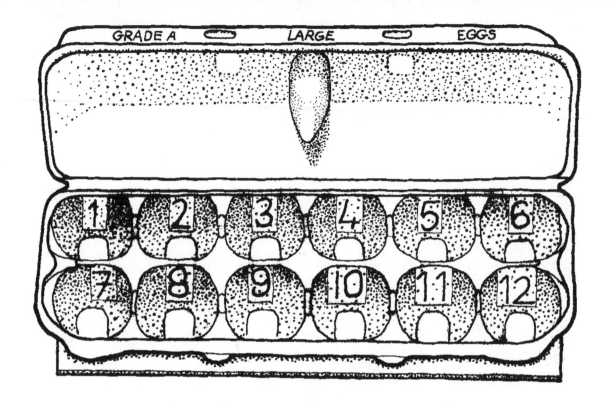

GRADE A · LARGE · EGGS

To Score:

12. The number in each cup is the cup's value. Add up the values of the cups where pennies have landed. For example, if there is one penny each in cups 2, 10, and 6, the score is 18 (2 + 10 + 6 = 18).

13. If there is one coin each in two cups that are in a column, like cups 1 and 7, 2 and 8, or 3 and 9, the values are multiplied by each other. For example, if there is a coin each in cups 1, 2, and 7, the score is 9 (1 × 7 + 2 = 9). Remember that you always multiply first, then add.

14. If there is more than one penny in two cups that are in a column, do not multiply. Just add the values of the cups together. For example, if there are two pennies in cups 4 and 10, and one penny in cup 5, the score is 33 (4 + 4 + 10 + 10 + 5 = 33).

15. The player who reaches 100 points first wins.

To Play:

8. Write the numbers 1 through 12 on the scrap paper. Cut out the numbers so they are each on a separate strip of paper, about 1 inch (2.5 cm) high. Glue the number strips into the egg cups, as shown.

9. Fold the flaps of the base up so they support the lid of the egg carton. Stand the lid of the carton up like a backboard.

10. Place the carton on the ground. Select a marker, such as a rock or a stick, and place it 6 feet (1.8 m) from the egg carton. Each player must stand behind the marker during his or her turn.

11. Each player tries to toss ten pennies into the carton. The carton lid can be used as a backboard. Use a pencil and paper to keep score.

Stacking Game

Collecting the pieces to play this game can be as much fun as the game itself. Use your imagination and put your recycling skills to the test.

Instructions

To Play:

1. Place the vinegar bottle on a flat, level surface. Lay the ruler flat across the top, slightly off-center.

2. The first player places the first object from the collection on the ruler without tipping the ruler.

3. Each player follows in turn until the ruler and everything on it topples.

4. Once an object is selected it cannot be exchanged.

5. Once the stack topples or the pieces are used up, the scores are tallied to determine the winner. Use a pencil and paper to keep score.

To Score:

6. You get 10 points if a piece is successfully placed without moving the ruler.

7. You get 5 points if a piece is successfully placed but the ruler was moved.

8. You lose 15 points if the ruler topples.

Note: It takes a steady hand and a lot of patience to win this game. Don't give up!

Team Toss Game

*Recycle a used soda-bottle carrier into a fun
tossing game you play in teams.*

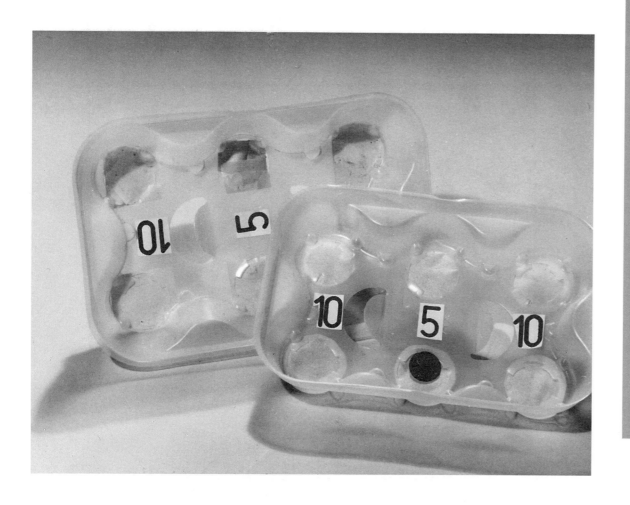

You Need

- ❏ white paper
- ❏ a hard plastic six-pack soda-bottle carrier (see the photo on this page)
- ❏ masking tape, 1½ inches (3.8 cm) wide

Have on Hand

- ❏ a marking pen
- ❏ a pad of paper
- ❏ a pencil
- ❏ stick glue
- ❏ ten pennies

Tools

- ❏ scissors

Instructions

1. Write the numbers 5, 10, and 10 on the white paper with the marking pen. Make each number about 1 inch (2.5 cm) high. Cut out the numbers with scissors.

2. Glue the numbers to the inside of the carrier, as shown.

3. Cut six 2-inch (5-cm) pieces of masking tape. Cover the top side of each of the six holes in the carrier with a piece of tape, so the sticky side faces the same way as the numbers.

To Play:

4. Form teams of two. One team member holds the carrier like a tray, through the finger holes, with the sticky side of the tape up.

5. The second team member stands 6 feet (1.8 m) from his or her teammate and tosses ten pennies, one at a time, at the carrier. The catcher can move the carrier to try to catch the pennies. The object is to get the pennies to stick to the masking tape.

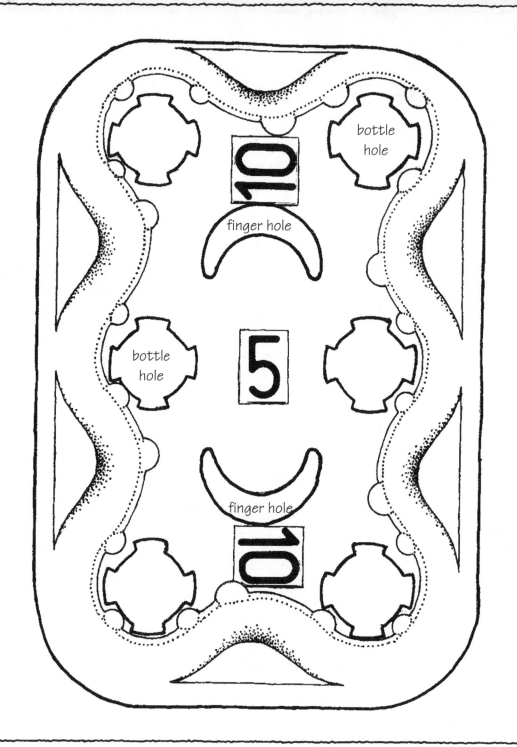

6. The second team plays after the first team has tossed all ten pennies and their score has been added up.

7. Teammates switch positions after each turn.

8. After each team has had five turns the game is complete. If there is a tie, extra turns may be taken until the tie is broken. Keep track of the score with a pencil and a pad of paper.

To Score:

9. For each coin that does not land in the tray, subtract 5 points from the score. It is possible to have a negative score.

10. At the end of one team's turn, all the coins stuck to the tape are scored according to the number written next to the tape. Coins that are in the carrier but not stuck to tape count as 0 points.

Recycling Facts & Tips

Did you know that:

- Each of us produces about 3½ pounds (1.3 kg) of garbage every day.

- Nearly 80% of all the garbage we create is buried in landfills.

How you can help:

- You **can** make a difference! The best way to stand up against the tide of trash is to **educate** and **organize**. Spread the word to your friends and neighbors. See page 127 for information about groups who can help.

Pinball

*Most pinball machines stop working if you tilt them,
but you have to tilt this handmade "machine" to make it work.*

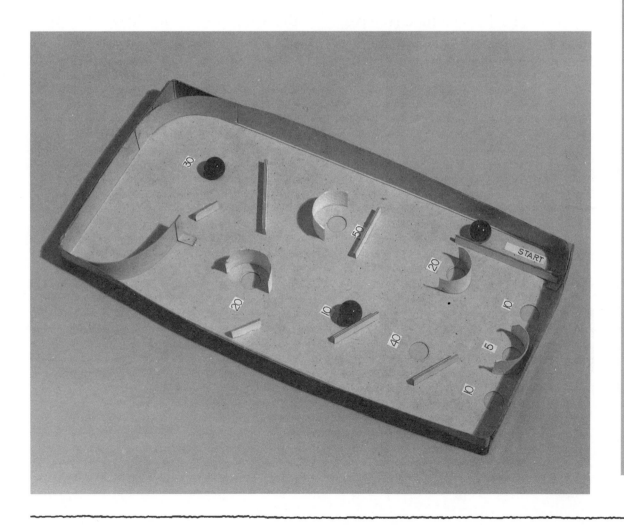

You Need

- ❏ heavy drawing paper,
  ¾ × 8 inches (1.9 × 20 cm)
- ❏ a large facial-tissue box,
  2 × 6 inches (5 × 15 cm)
- ❏ heavy cardboard, such as
  the back of a legal pad
- ❏ three small marbles

Have on Hand

- ❏ a bowl of warm water
- ❏ a marking pen
- ❏ paper towels
- ❏ several rubber bands
- ❏ stick glue
- ❏ white glue

Tools

- ❏ a dime
- ❏ a pencil
- ❏ a pushpin
- ❏ a ruler
- ❏ scissors
- ❏ several paper clips

Instructions

1. Wet the heavy paper completely by soaking it in the bowl of water for a minute. Wipe off excess water with a paper towel.

2. Wrap the wet paper around the glue stick. Put a rubber band around the paper to hold it in place. Put the stick aside for the paper to dry (you may need to let it dry overnight).

3. Mark the outside of the tissue box in two places on each side, 1 inch (2.5 cm) up from the bottom. Use the ruler and pencil to draw lines on each side connecting the marks you have just made.

4. Use the Pushpin Method (see page 12) and scissors to cut along the lines you have just drawn.

5. Use the dime as a guide to draw nine circles on the inside of the cutoff bottom of the tissue box. The positions of the circles should be similar to those in the diagram on page 45, but they do not need to be exact. The circles at the bottom of the box (near the word START) should not be closer than ¼ inch (.6 cm) to the side.

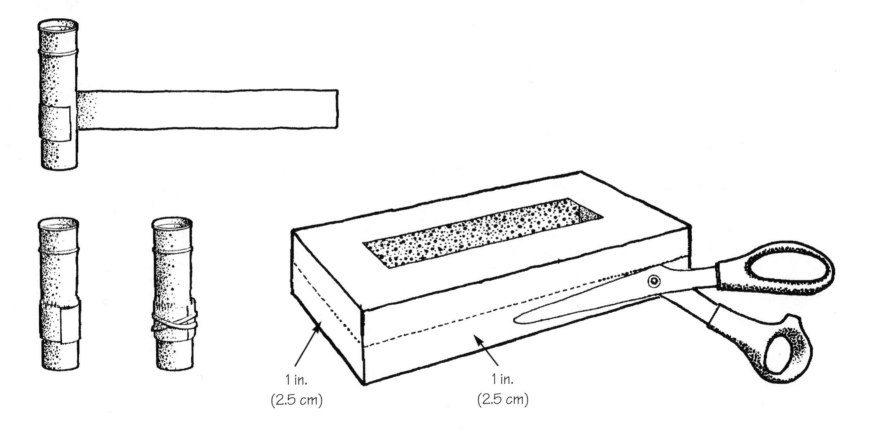

1 in.
(2.5 cm)

1 in.
(2.5 cm)

6. Use the Pushpin Method and scissors to cut out the circles you have just marked.

7. Use the marking pen to write in the word START and the numbers, as shown on page 45.

8. Use the scissors to cut three strips of cardboard from the cutoff top of the tissue box: two that are 1 × 3 inches (2.5 × 7.5 cm), and one that is ¼ × 1¼ inches (.6 × 3 cm).

9. Glue one of the long pieces of cardboard in a curve across the top right corner, as shown. Hold the strip in place with paper clips while the glue dries.

10. Fold ¼ inch (.6 cm) of one end of the small piece of cardboard over to make a foot. Glue the long part of this piece to the end of one long piece. Hold the pieces together with a paper clip for 20 minutes while the glue dries.

11. Glue the piece you assembled in step **10** into the top left corner of the box, as shown.

a. Make sure to put glue on the bottom of the "foot" of the smaller piece. Stick a pushpin through

the foot and into the bottom of the box to hold the foot in place while the glue dries.

b. Use a paper clip to hold the other end of the strip in place against the side of the box.

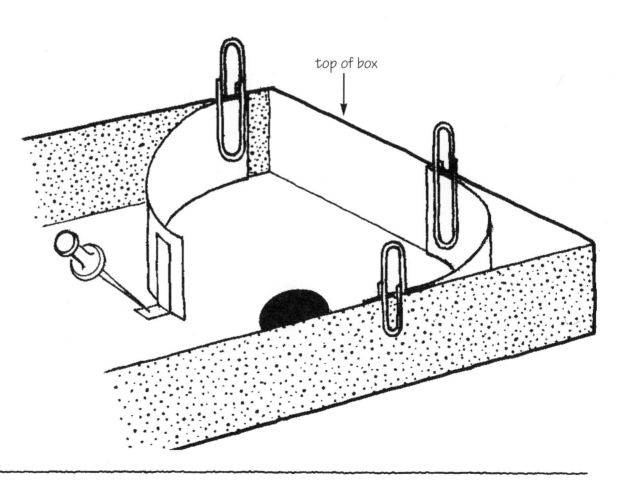

top of box

12. Cut seven pieces of heavy cardboard. Each one should be ¼ inch (.6 cm) high. Cut:

two pieces 1¼ inches (3 cm) long
one piece 1½ inches (3.8 cm) long
two pieces ¾ inch (1.9 cm) long
one piece 2¼ inches (5.6 cm) long
one piece 3 inches (7.5 cm) long

13. Glue one edge of each of the pieces you have just cut to the bottom of the box in the positions shown on page 45.

14. When the heavy paper you worked with in step **2** has dried completely, remove the rubber band. The paper should spring open but remain curled.

15. Cut four half circles from the curled heavy paper. Glue the half circles into place, as shown on page 45. Let the glue dry for at least 20 minutes.

To Play:

16. Place one or more marbles in the START chute. Tilt the board so that the marbles roll out of the chute. Tip and tilt the board until you have all of the marbles in holes. The person with the highest score wins.

✪ **Even Better:** To make the game harder, remove the small cardboard bars and the paper half circles.

Recycling Facts & Tips

Did you know that:

- More than 73 million tons (66 million t) of paper are made each year.

- Paper is the largest single part of the waste we produce.

How you can help:

- Recycling isn't only about reducing garbage, it's also about reducing pollution. Recycling one newspaper every day for a year can prevent nearly 14 pounds (6.3 kg) of air pollution.

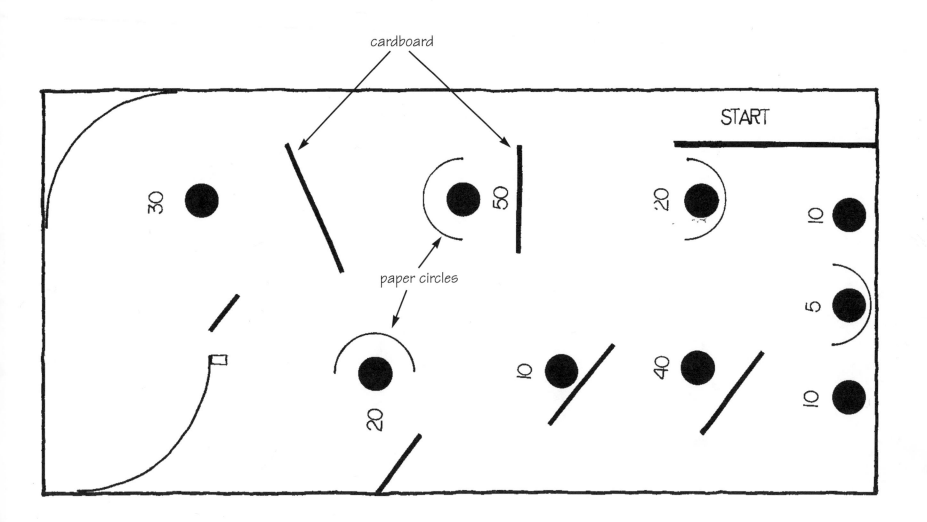

Gardening

Miniature Planters

*Recycle tiny containers to start a collection of small plants.
Try to see how many different and unique containers
you can come up with. Use your imagination!*

You Need

- ❏ several small containers, one for each plant (some examples of items you could use: an odd coffee cup, shot glasses, small measuring cups, etc.)
- ❏ small pebbles
- ❏ potting soil
- ❏ coarse sand (not fine beach sand)
- ❏ small cactus plants
- ❏ an old tray or aluminum pan that will hold water

(continued on page 50)

Have on Hand

- ❑ gloves (to handle cacti)
- ❑ a measuring cup
- ❑ an old pan or mixing bowl
- ❑ water

Tools

- ❑ an old spoon
- ❑ a pencil with a sharp point
- ❑ a pushpin

Instructions

1. Separate the glass, hard plastic, or metal containers from the soft plastic ones.

2. Place a layer of small pebbles on the bottom of the glass, hard plastic, or metal containers.

3. Use the pushpin to make three or four drainage holes in the bottom of the soft plastic containers. Enlarge the holes with a pencil point.

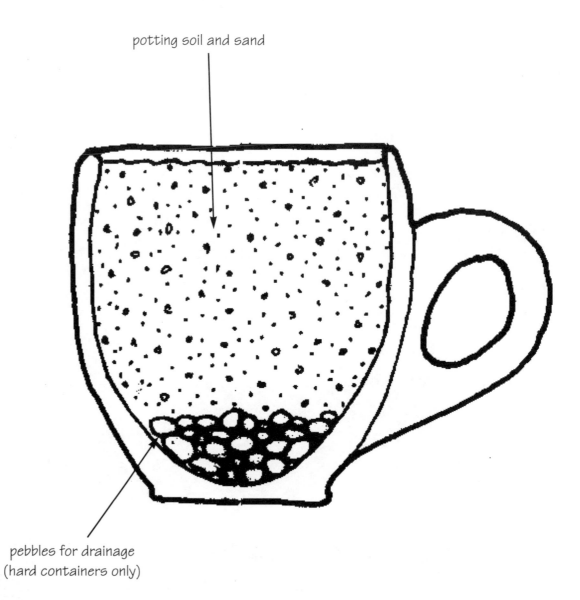

potting soil and sand

pebbles for drainage
(hard containers only)

4. Use the spoon to mix two cups (0.5 liter) of potting soil with one cup (0.25 liter) of coarse sand in an old pan.

5. Spoon the mixture into each planter until the planters are nearly full.

6. Plant a small plant in each planter. Press the soil down softly.

7. Water each plant and place them on the tray or pan. Place the plants outdoors when the weather is warm or indoors near a window when it gets cold.

Note: Only water the cacti when the soil is dry. They should **not** be watered often.

Scarecrow

Scarecrows are used to keep birds away from plants and vegetables. Use some old clothes and newspaper to make this friendly garden guardian.

You Need

- ❏ five plastic grocery bags
- ❏ newspaper
- ❏ a worn-out adjustable cap
- ❏ a worn-out pair of gloves
- ❏ a worn-out long-sleeve T-shirt (kid sized)
- ❏ two pieces of 1 × 2-inch (2.5 × 5-cm) soft wood (like pine), one 2 feet (60 cm) long, and the other 5 feet (1.3 m) long

Note: Wood is sold in different sizes. Some of the sizes are slightly different from the actual measurements of the wood. The wood you need for this project is called 1 × 2, even though its measurements are slightly smaller than that.

- ❏ a worn-out pair of pants (kid sized)
- ❏ black paper

(continued on page 54)

Have on Hand

- ❏ black button thread
- ❏ double-sided tape
- ❏ duct tape
- ❏ masking tape
- ❏ safety pins
- ❏ tape
- ❏ two 1¼-inch (3-cm) screws

Tools

- ! a wood saw
- ❏ scissors
- ❏ a screwdriver

Instructions

To Make the Head:

1. Flatten a plastic grocery bag so the sides are tucked in between the front and back, and tape the sides in place with masking tape, as shown. Make sure there is no tape on the bag handles.

2. Fold the bottom corners of the bag over onto the front and tape them down with masking tape, as shown.

3. Fold the bottom of the areas you have just folded again and tape them down with masking tape, as shown.

4. Tear some newspaper into 4-inch (10-cm) -wide strips. Crumple the strips and stuff them into the plastic bag. The bag should be full enough to hold the cap in place.

5. Push the newspaper toward the bottom of the bag until there is only about 3 inches (7.5 cm) of space left in the bag. Squeeze the top 4 inches (10 cm) of the bag where there is paper together to make a neck. Wrap this part of the bag with masking tape.

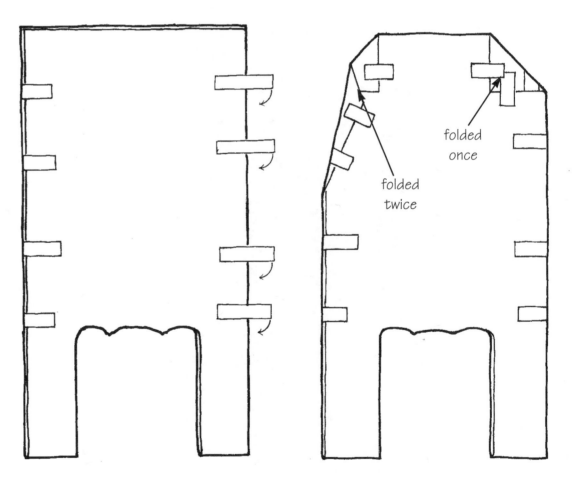

folded once

folded twice

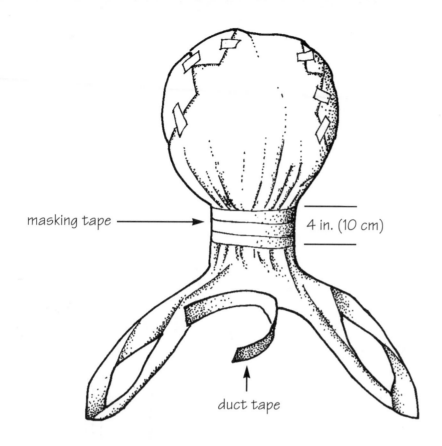

masking tape

4 in. (10 cm)

duct tape

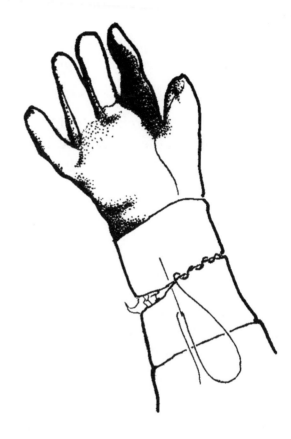

6. Tear a 12-inch (30-cm) piece of duct tape in half lengthwise. Place one piece of it around the bottom of the neck, between the handles, on both the front and back. Set the head aside.

To Make the Hands:

7. Tear some newspaper into strips 1 inch (2.5 cm) wide.

8. Crumple one strip at a time and stuff it into the fingers of the gloves. Use the eraser end of a pencil to push it all the way in if you are having trouble.

9. Once the fingers are stuffed, stuff the rest of the gloves with crumpled newspaper.

10. Stuff the arms of the T-shirt with newspaper strips 3 inches (7.5 cm) wide.

To Assemble the Scarecrow:

11. Thread the black button thread through the needle. Use the Whip-Stitch Method (see page 16) to sew the cuffs of the gloves to the cuffs of the T-shirt.

12. Use the Whip-Stitch Method to sew the collar of the shirt to the edge of the neck that is covered with duct tape.

13. Slip the arms of the T-shirt through the handles of the head bag. Arrange the handles so they are looped around the armpits of the shirt.

! 14. Ask an **adult helper** to saw one end of the 5-foot (1.5-m) piece of wood into a point.

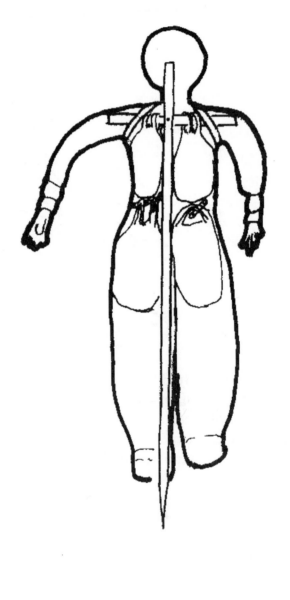

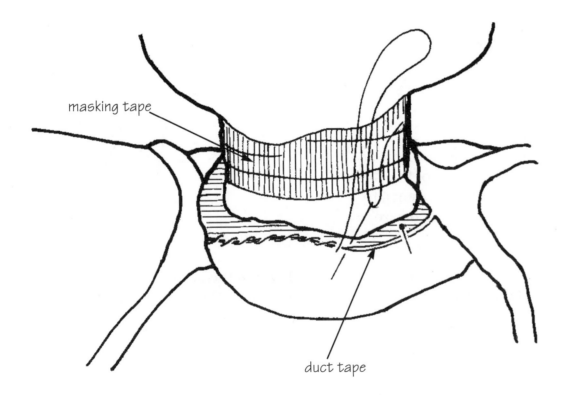

masking tape

duct tape

18. Tie two of the bags onto the shorter piece of wood, one on each side, as shown. Pull the shirt over the bags.

19. Use safety pins to attach two bags inside the top back of the pants.

20. Put the upright stick through one leg of the pants. Use the safety pins to pin the top of the pants to the T-shirt.

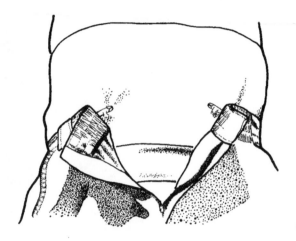

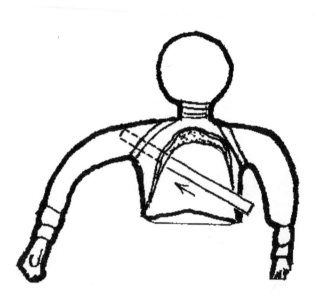

15. Insert the 2-foot (60-cm) piece of wood into the arms of the T-shirt.

! 16. Insert the 5-foot (1.3-m) piece of wood into the T-shirt and into the head. Ask an **adult** to screw the two pieces of wood together with two screws.

17. Stuff four more shopping bags with newspaper.

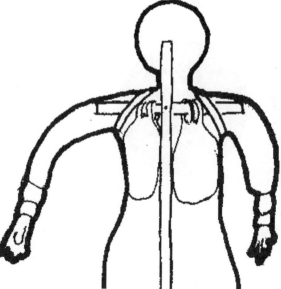

21. Draw the Face Pattern (page 58) on the black paper with a pencil. Cut the face parts out with scissors. Use the double-sided tape to glue the features to the front of the head.

22. Stick the scarecrow into the ground by pushing the pointed end of the stick into the ground. Put the cap on the scarecrow's head.

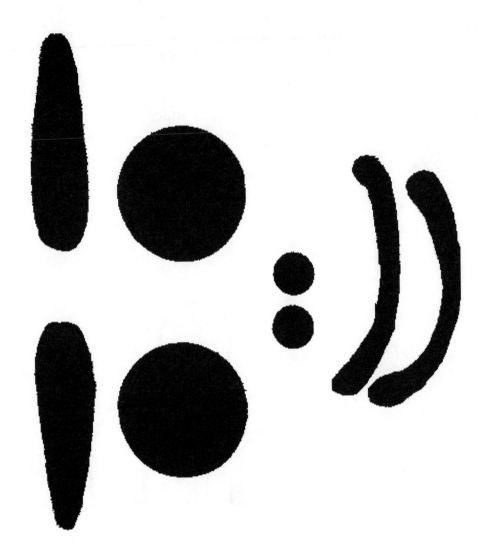

Plant Starters

Use plastic soda bottles to keep tender, young plants protected from cold nights, animals, and other dangers.

You Need

- ❏ clear plastic soft-drink bottles, ½-liter to 3-liter size, one for every two plants

Have on Hand

- ❏ masking tape

Tools

- ❏ a pushpin
- ❏ scissors

Instructions

1. Wash each bottle out and remove any labels. Replace the bottle caps.

2. Wrap a piece of masking tape around the middle of each bottle.

3. Use the Pushpin Method (see page 12) to cut each bottle in half along one edge of the tape. Keep both halves of the bottles.

4. Use the pushpin to punch several holes in all of the bottle halves. This is so that the plants can breathe.

To Use the Plant Starters:

5. Plant your young sprouts outdoors in the spring.

6. For each plant, choose a starter that is large enough to completely cover the plant, with a little room at the top for the plant to grow.

7. Cover each sprout with a starter. Make sure to press the edges of the starter firmly into the ground so it doesn't blow away.

8. The starters may be removed when the weather is warm enough and the plants are large enough to fend for themselves.

Note: When the starters have been removed, don't forget that you may need to tie the plants to stakes, or put small fences around them to protect them while they grow.

Bird Feeder

This easy-to-make bird feeder will attract birds to your yard.
Remember that once you start feeding birds you need
to keep feeding them, and that they will expect
food in the same place every day.

You Need

- ❑ a small juice carton, 16 fl. oz. (473 ml) size
- ❑ two pieces of heavy string, 36 inches (90 cm) long
- ❑ two Styrofoam meat trays, 9 × 7 inches (22.5 × 17.5 cm)
- ❑ pebbles or sand
- ❑ a long piece of rope
- ❑ birdseed

Have on Hand

- ❑ scrap paper
- ❑ white glue

Tools

- ❑ a pencil with a sharp point
- ❑ a pushpin
- ❑ scissors

Instructions

1. Make a small puddle of white glue on a piece of scrap paper. Dip 1 inch (2.5 cm) of each end of both pieces of string into the glue. Wipe off any extra glue with your fingers, and hang the ends of the string over the edge of a table to dry.

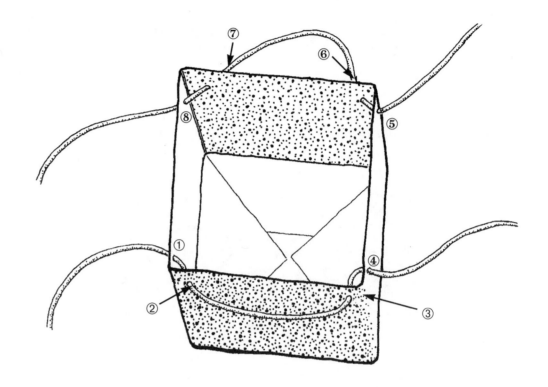

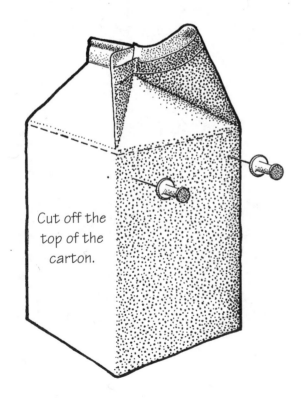

Cut off the top of the carton.

2. Rinse out the juice carton. Use the Pushpin Method (see page 12) and scissors to cut off the top of the juice carton. Discard the cutoff top.

3. Use the pushpin to make eight holes in the sides of the carton. The holes should be ½ inch (1.3 cm) down from the top edge of the carton, and ¼ inch (.6 cm) in from the corners, as shown.

4. Use the pencil point to enlarge the holes so that the string will pass through easily.

5. Starting anywhere, label the holes 1 to 8 with a pencil.

6. Push one end of one piece of string into hole #1, out through hole #2, across one side of the carton, in through hole #3, and out again through hole #4. Pull enough string through so that there is the same amount of extra string on both ends.

7. Repeat step **6** for holes #5 through #8 with the second piece of string.

8. Wash and dry the Styrofoam trays. Place one Styrofoam tray inside the other. Hold them together firmly.

9. Use the pushpin to make a hole in each corner of the bottom of the trays. Make the holes starting from the top tray, and make sure to push through both trays.

10. Use the pencil point to enlarge the holes so that two pieces of string will pass through them easily.

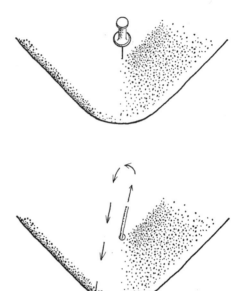

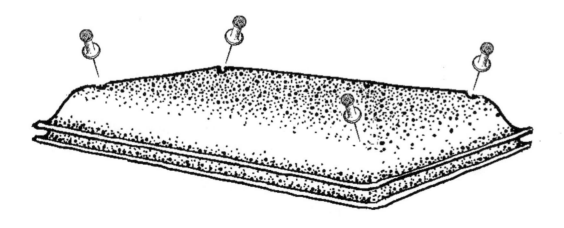

11. Pass one end of string from the juice carton up through one of the holes in the trays. Wrap the string around the edge of the trays and push it up through the same hole again. The carton should be as far away from the tray as the tray is from the loose string ends.

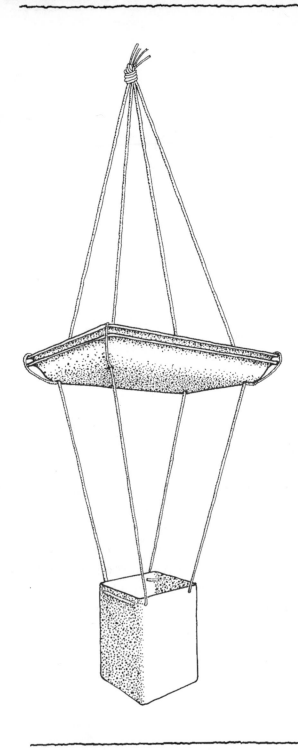

12. Repeat step **11** with the other three ends of string. Make sure that the carton hangs straight below the trays when you hold them up by the four loose string ends.

13. Tie the loose string ends together.

14. Fill the carton about three-quarters of the way up with sand or pebbles.

To Hang the Feeder

15. Select a sturdy tree for the feeder. If possible, choose a tree you can see from your house so you can watch the birds eating.

16. Throw the rope over a low tree branch. Make sure that the branch is strong enough to support the weight of the feeder. If you aren't sure, ask an **adult** to help you select a branch.

17. Tie the feeder to one end of the rope.

18. Pull the other end of the rope until the feeder is low enough so that it's easy to put birdseed in it, but high enough so that animals on the ground can't get it.

19. Tie the other end of the rope around the trunk of the tree.

20. Fill the feeder with birdseed.

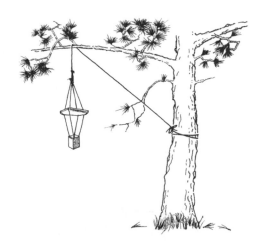

✪ **Even Better:** Have an **adult** help you find out what birds live in your area and what kinds of seeds they like best.

Bug Trap

Get rid of pesky garden insects! This simple bug trap will allow you to capture insects without using chemicals.

Instructions

1. Arrange the three bottle tops upside down on the plate in a triangle so they will support the jar upside-down. Make sure the jar can stand on its own.

2. Remove the jar and mark the positions of the caps with a pencil.

3. Use the double-sided tape to stick the caps to the plate.

4. Use double-sided tape to stick the jug top to the plate, in the middle of the triangle made by the other three caps.

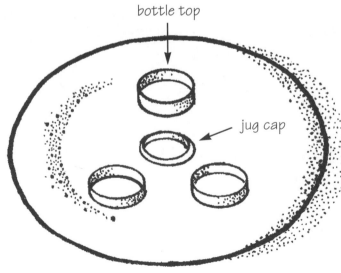

bottle top

jug cap

5. Place a dollop of honey in the jug cap.

6. Place the plate where it will not be disturbed. Place the jar upside down on the caps. Insects will eat the honey, fly up into the upside-down jar, and be trapped.

7. Wash the jar out regularly.

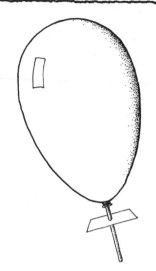

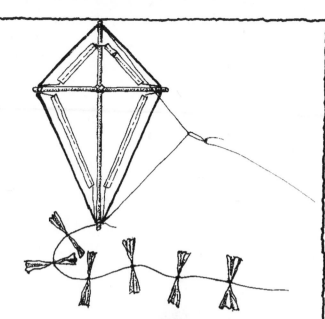

Other Outdoor Fun

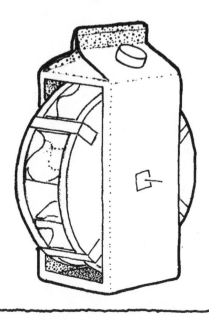

Jet Balloon

*If you let a blown-up balloon go, it flies around
all over the place. But if you add these fins,
the balloon will fly straight and fast!*

You Need

- ❏ a plastic drinking straw
- ❏ a balloon
- ❏ a rubber band
- ❏ an old index card,
  postcard, or magazine
  subscription card,
  1½ × 3 inches (3.8 × 7.5 cm)

Tools

- ❏ a pencil
- ❏ a ruler
- ❏ scissors

Instructions

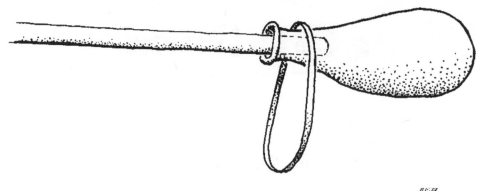

1. Use the scissors to cut the drinking straw in half.

2. Pinch one end of one half of the straw and insert it into one end of the other half. Carefully push the first half completely inside the second half.

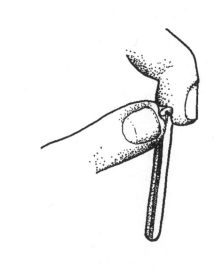

3. Place the mouth of the balloon over one end of the doubled straw.

4. Loop the rubber band around the mouth of the balloon several times, until it's tight.

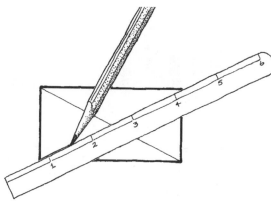

5. Use the pencil and ruler to draw lines on the card from corner to corner. The point where the lines cross is the center of the card. Make a small hole with the pushpin in the exact center of the card.

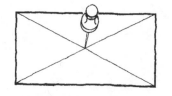

6. Enlarge the hole with the pencil point so the straw will just fit and stay in place. Push the free end of the straw through the hole until the card is three-quarters of the way up the straw.

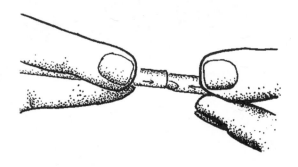

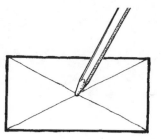

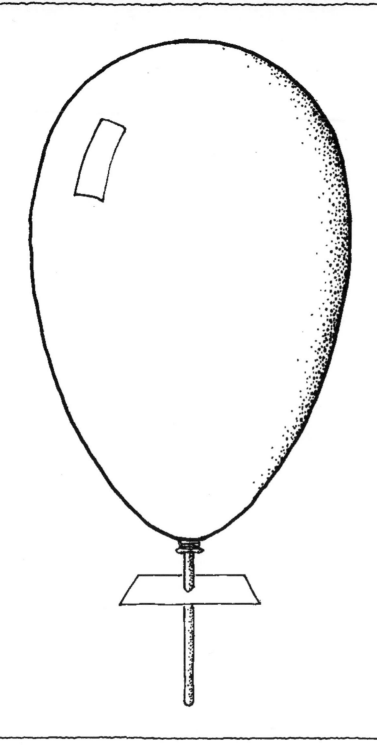

To Make the Balloon Fly:

7. Blow up the balloon through the straw.

8. When the balloon is full, place your finger over the straw.

9. Release the jet balloon and watch it sail away. Each jet balloon will fly a little differently.

✪ **Even Better:** Try bending the card in various shapes, as shown, to change the way the balloon flies.

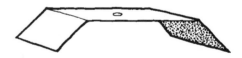

Boomerang

Throw this boomerang at any angle and it should return to you.

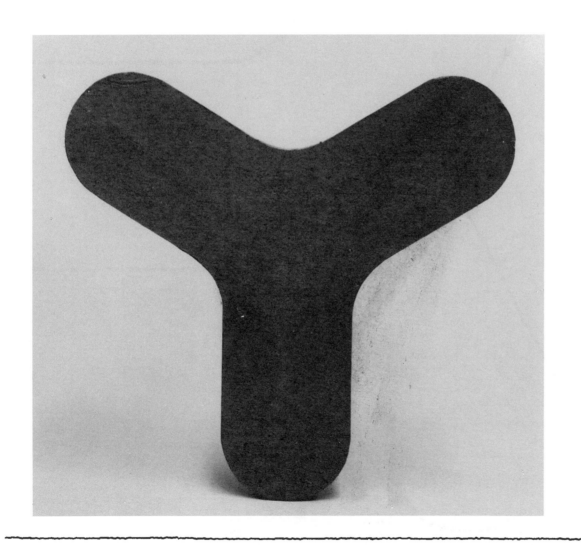

Instructions

To Make the Boomerang:

1. Use the Transfer Method (see page 13) to transfer the Boomerang Pattern onto the cardboard.

2. Use scissors to cut out the cardboard boomerang: First, cut roughly all the way around the outline of the boomerang. Then carefully cut along the edges of the boomerang.

To Throw the Boomerang:

3. Use your boomerang outdoors when there isn't any wind; it's too light to work when it's windy out.

4. Start with the boomerang in your hand, behind your shoulder. Throw it overhand and watch it come back to you. It may take you a few tries to learn how to throw it, so keep practicing!

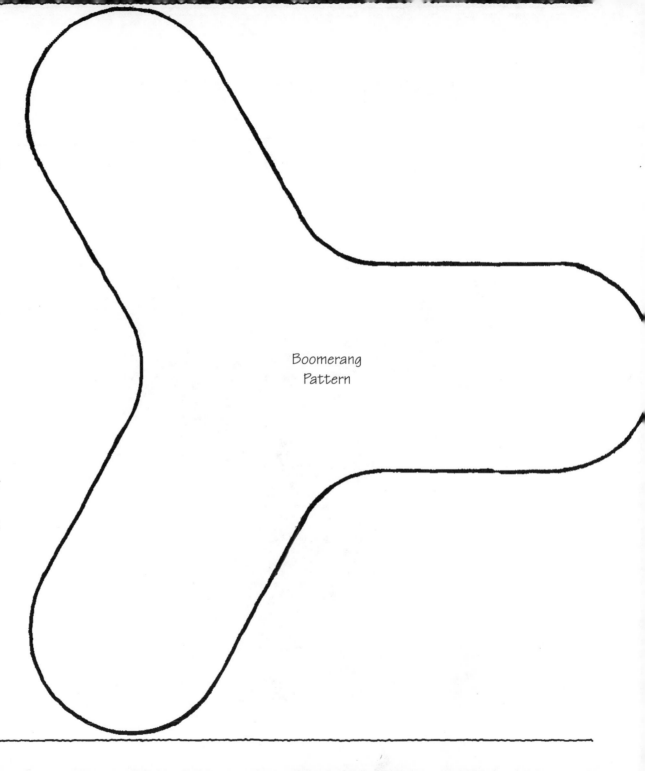

Boomerang
Pattern

Kite

Recycle some old drinking straws and plastic shopping bags to make a high-flying kite, perfect for a windy day at the beach or in your favorite park.

You Need

- ☐ ten drinking straws
- ☐ four plastic vegetable or fruit bags, 12 × 14 inches (30 × 35 cm)
- ☐ one plastic shopping bag
- ☐ a roll of string, at least 150 feet (45 m) long

Have on Hand

- ☐ a permanent marking pen
- ☐ strapping tape or other strong tape
- ☐ transparent tape

Tools

- ☐ a ruler
- ☐ scissors

Instructions

To Make the Struts:

1. Pinch one end of a straw and push it halfway into another straw.

2. Add four more straws so that the strut is 24 inches (60 cm) long.

3. Cut one straw in half. Completely insert one half into each end of the long strut you have just made.

4. Repeat steps **1** through **3** to assemble the remaining straws into a 16-inch (40-cm) strut.

5. Cross the struts so the shorter strut is centered 8 inches (20 cm) from one end of the longer strut. Tape the two struts together in this position with strapping tape. The joint will be stronger and easier to make if you use thin strips of tape instead of one wide piece.

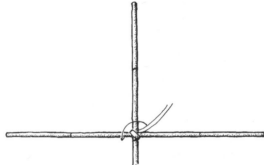

6. Wrap pieces of strapping tape ½ inch (1.3 cm) from the ends of each strut.

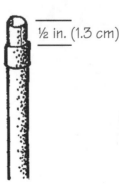

½ in. (1.3 cm)

7. Use the scissors to cut two slots opposite each other in both ends of each strut. Cut from the end of the strut up to the tape you wrapped around the struts in step **6**. These slots will hold the string that frames the kite.

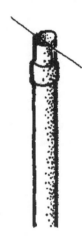

To Frame the Kite:

8. Cut 12 feet (36 m) of string. Slip one end of the string into the slits in the bottom of the long strut (the bottom is the end furthest from the joint with the shorter strut).

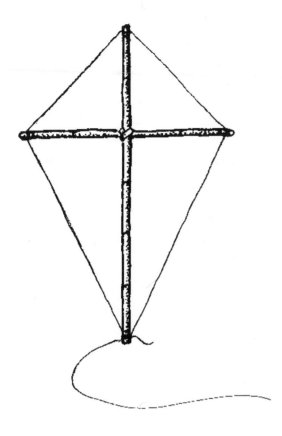

11. Use the scissors to cut open the plastic grocery bag. Cut down the sides, and cut off the bottom seam entirely.

12. Cut off the handles.

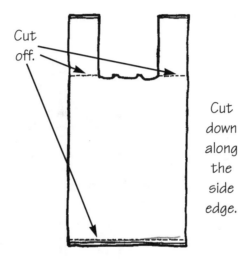

Cut off.

Cut down along the side edge.

15. Lay the ruler along one side of the frame and mark the plastic along the **outside** of the ruler. Repeat on the other three sides of the frame.

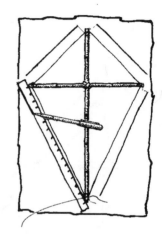

16. Use the scissors to cut the plastic bag along the lines you have just marked.

9. Stretch the string around the kite from strut to strut, placing it in the slots as you go along.

10. When you get back to where the string starts, tie the loose end to the string. Do not cut off the extra string; it will be the tail.

13. Pull out the sides of the bag and cut along the crease down one side.

To Assemble the Kite:

14. Open the bag and flatten it on the work surface. Center the kite frame on the plastic.

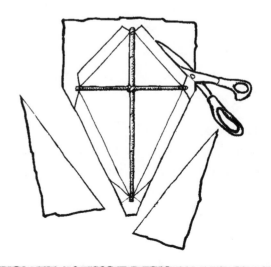

17. Place the frame back on the plastic and cut the corners as shown.

18. Fold the plastic over the string edges of the frame and tape the plastic together, as shown.

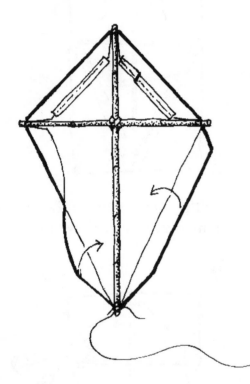

19. Flatten out each fruit and vegetable bag on the work surface. Cut the bags into thirds. Tie the nine pieces of plastic onto the tail.

20. Cut a 48-inch (120-cm) length of string. Tie it to the top and bottom of the long strut. Place a piece of strapping tape over the place where the string is connected to the strut.

21. Tie the loose end of the ball of string to the piece of string you have just tied to the kite. Tie it securely so your kite doesn't fly away!

✪ **Even Better:** If the kite dives to the ground, make the tail longer. If the kite consistently drifts to the ground, make the tail shorter.

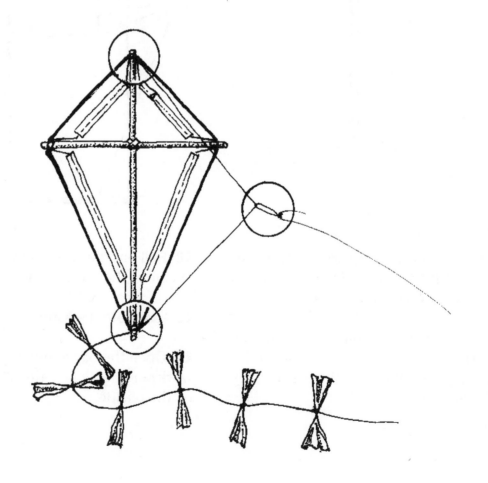

Roll-Back Toy

*Here's a toy that's pretty hard to lose. Roll it on the sidewalk
or floor and watch it roll back to you.*

Instructions

1. Use the Center-Finding Method (see page 15) to find the center of the lid and bottom of the oats carton.

2. Use the ruler and pencil to draw a straight line through each center mark. Make marks on the line ¼ inch (.6 cm) on each side of the center mark, as shown.

3. Make holes with the pushpin at the two pairs of points you have just marked. Do not make holes through the center marks. Enlarge each hole with the pencil point.

4. Link two rubber bands together, as shown.

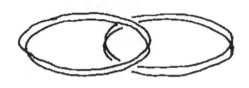

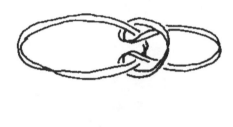

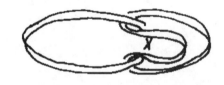

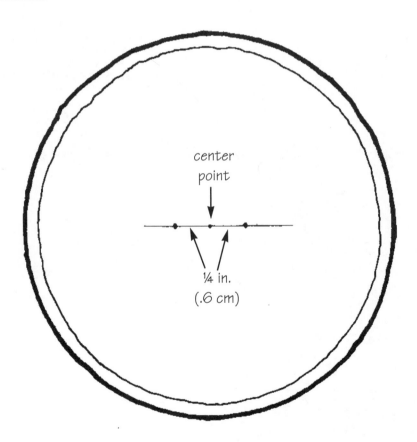

center point

¼ in.
(.6 cm)

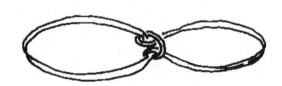

5. From the outside of the bottom of the carton, use the pencil point to push one of the linked rubber bands though one hole. Pull the rubber band through the hole, up to the knot. If you are having trouble, use a paper clip bent into a hook to grab the rubber band.

6. Push the other end of the linked rubber band through the other hole in the bottom of the carton.

7. Inside the carton, use the method shown in step **4** to link one rubber band to each end of the rubber band that you pushed through the bottom of the carton.

8. Push one end of one of the rubber bands through the nut twice. Adjust the position of the nut so that when the rubber band is stretched to the top of the carton, the nut is in the middle of the carton.

9. Push one end of the rubber bands though one of the holes in the carton lid. Slip the toothpick through the loop of the rubber band to hold it in place outside the lid.

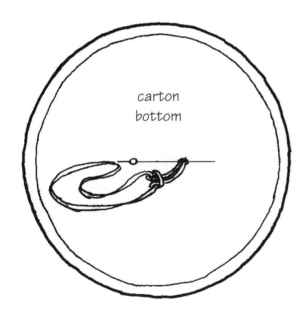

carton
bottom

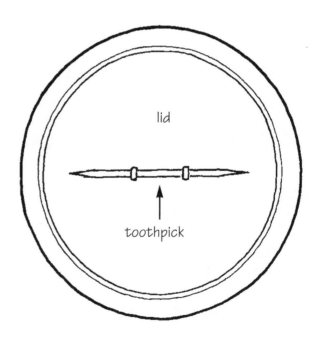

lid

toothpick

10. Repeat step **9** with the other end of the rubber bands.

11. Replace the lid on the carton and twist it so the toothpick on the lid and the line of rubber band on the bottom of the carton are parallel.

12. Roll the carton away on a smooth, level surface and watch it stop and roll back to you.

Note: If your roll-back toy doesn't work, the problem may be due to one or more of these three things:

> **1.** The nut may not be heavy enough.
>
> **2.** The rubber bands may be too elastic.
>
> **3.** The rubber bands may be too stiff.

Experiment with these three factors until the carton returns to you. Be patient—it may take a while before you get the right combination.

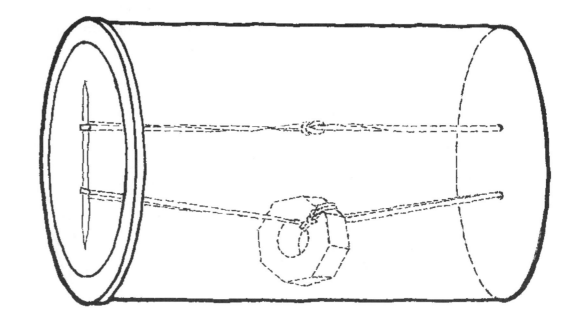

Sundial

A sundial tells time using shadows cast by the sun. Set your sundial in the ground outside so you can always know when to go home for supper!

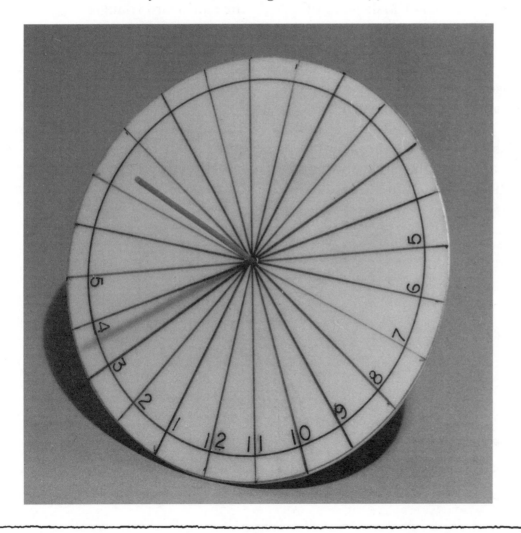

You Need

❑ a piece of cardboard, such as from the back of an old pad of paper or a cereal box
❑ a Styrofoam meat or vegetable tray, at least 7 inches (17.5 cm) square
❑ a bamboo skewer

Have on Hand

❑ glue
❑ a pencil with a sharp point
❑ a permanent marking pen
❑ a pushpin
❑ tape

Tools

❑ a ruler
❑ scissors

Instructions

1. Wash and dry the Styrofoam tray.

2. Use the Transfer Method (see page 13) to transfer the Sundial Pattern (page 85) onto the Styrofoam tray.

3. Use the scissors to cut out the sundial from the Styrofoam tray.

4. Darken the pattern lines on the Styrofoam sundial with a marking pen.

To Make the Cardboard Base:

5. For the sundial to work, it has to be tilted at the correct angle. The angle depends on where on the planet you live. Ask your parents or a teacher what latitude you live at. Round the number to the closest 10; for example, if you live at 42 latitude, round to 40; if you live at 49 latitude, round to 50.

6. Transfer the Base Pattern for the latitude you live at onto the cardboard.

7. Use the Pushpin Method (see page 17) to cut out the cardboard triangle.

To Mount the Sundial:

8. Wash and dry the bamboo skewer.

9. Tape the skewer to the top of the cardboard triangle (as pictured in the diagram below). Make sure that 2½ inches (6.3 cm) of the skewer stick out below the triangle.

10. Use a pushpin to make a hole in the center of the Styrofoam circle.

11. Insert the skewer through the circle and push the circle down until it rests on the front of the cardboard.

12. Insert the back end of the skewer (the end behind the sundial's face) into the ground. It's OK if the sundial doesn't rest flat against the edge of the cardboard triangle.

13. Ask an adult to help you find out which direction is true north. Point the end of the skewer north.

14. On a sunny day at noon, make sure that the shadow of the skewer falls directly on the 12 line on the face of the sundial. Your sundial is ready.

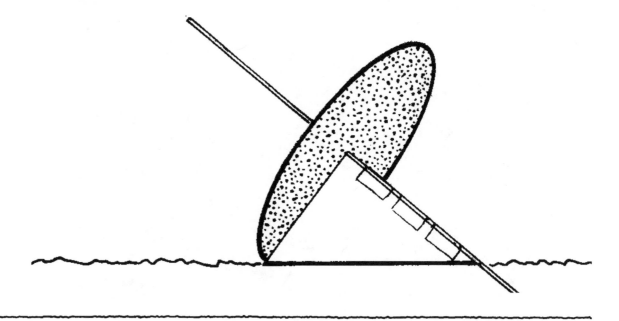

Sundial Pattern

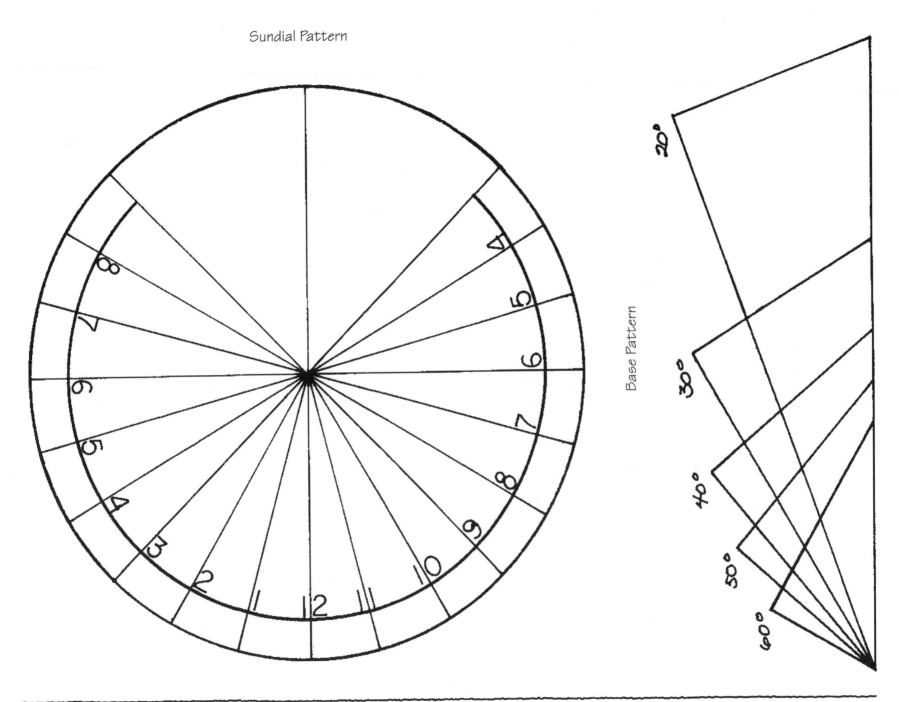

Base Pattern

The Screamer

Some people can imitate animal calls so well that even the animals are fooled. Try out this animal–noise maker and see what animals you can talk to.

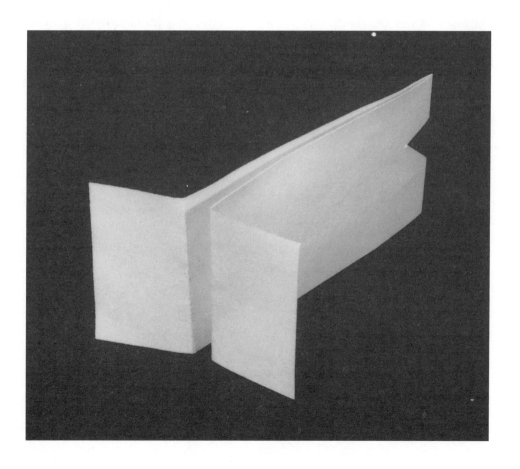

You Need

❏ scrap paper, either news-paper or typing paper

Tools

❏ scissors

Instructions

1. Cut a piece of paper roughly 1½ × 6 inches (3.8 × 15 cm).

2. Fold the strip in half from end to end.

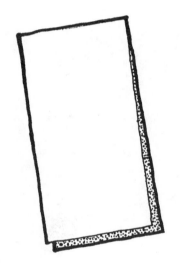

3. Fold a "foot" at the end of each half of the paper. These "feet" are just for you to hold on to, so they don't need to be an exact size.

4. Use the scissors to cut a V-shaped notch in the middle fold of the paper.

5. Hold the screamer between two fingers, with the feet facing in toward the palm of your hand.

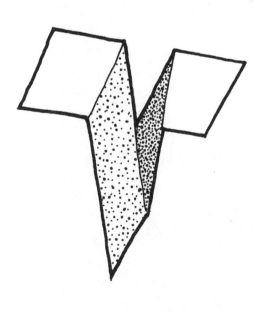

6. Hold the feet of the screamer to your lips and blow. If it doesn't make noise, you may need to hold it more loosely between your fingers. It may take a little practice.

✪ **Even Better:** You will get different noises if you experiment with different kinds of paper and different sizes of notches.

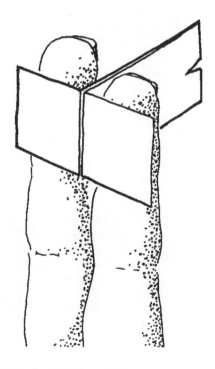

Waterwheel

Use a recycled juice carton and an egg carton to make a waterwheel you can place under a hose or under a downspout on a rainy day. Be sure not to waste water—try your Waterwheel on a rainy day.

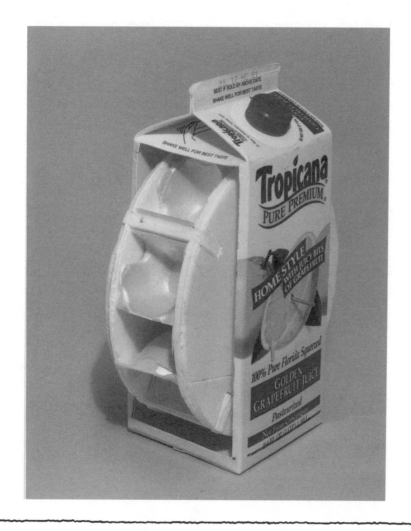

Instructions

To Make the Base:

1. Rinse out the juice carton.

2. On one side of the carton, use the ruler and marking pen to mark a panel whose edges are ¼ inch (.6 cm) in from the top, bottom, and sides of the carton. Do the same on the opposite side of the carton.

3. Use the Pushpin Method (see page 12) to cut out the panels you have just marked. Save the cutout pieces.

To Make the Wheel:

4. Wash and dry the Styrofoam trays.

5. With the scissors, cut off the rims of all the Styrofoam trays. Discard the cutoff pieces.

6. Use the Transfer Method (see page 13) to transfer the Wheel Pattern (page 94) onto each of the four pieces of Styrofoam.

7. Use the Pushpin Method and scissors to cut out all four Styrofoam wheels.

8. Use Styrofoam glue to stick two of the Styrofoam wheels together. Repeat with the other two wheels. Make sure to line up the slots on the Styrofoam wheels.

9. Use the scissors to cut eight ¾ × 2½-inch (1.9 × 6.3-cm) pieces from the scrap Styrofoam.

10. Glue the Styrofoam pieces together in pairs. These will be wheel supports.

11. Insert the bamboo skewer through the center holes of the wheels.

12. Move the two wheels apart on the skewer so that a wheel support fits in one pair of slots, with the outside edges of the support flush with the outside edges of the Styrofoam wheels. Insert the four supports into the four slots of the two wheels. If the supports aren't snug in the slots, use a little Styrofoam glue to keep them in place.

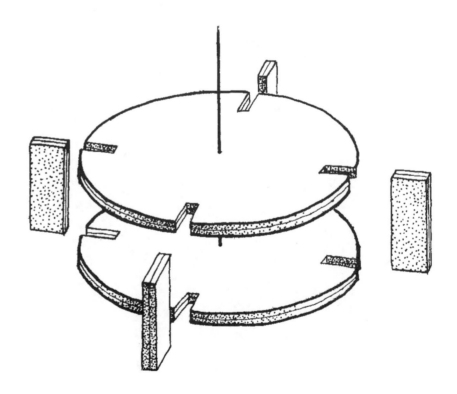

13. Carefully remove the skewer from the two wheels.

14. Neatly cut the lid and the front flaps off of the egg carton.

15. Cut the bottom of the egg carton into individual egg cups. Discard the four end cups. You will need only eight cups.

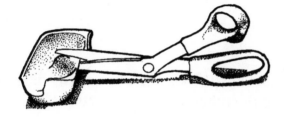

16. Glue the flat sides of two egg cups to either side of one of the wheel supports. Press them to the supports firmly so the glue sets. Repeat with the other three wheel supports.

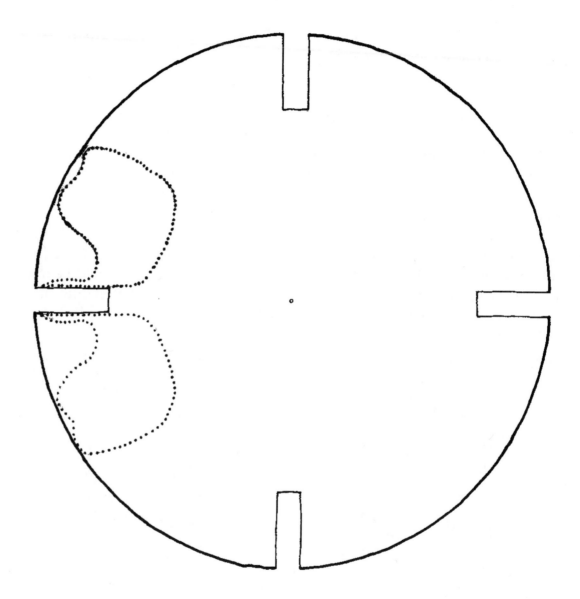

17. Cut four ½-inch (1.3-cm) -square pieces from the scrap cardboard left from the juice carton.

18. Use the pushpin to make a hole in the center of each square. Enlarge each hole slightly with the pointed tip of the skewer. These will be axle stops.

To Put the Wheel and Base Together:

19. On one side of the juice carton, measure a spot that is halfway across the carton and 4 inches (10 cm) down from the top of the side panel. Make a pushpin hole at this spot. Repeat on the opposite side.

20. Slip one axle stop onto the skewer so that it is 1 inch (2.5 cm) from the flat end of the skewer.

21. Insert the pointed end of the skewer through one of the holes you have just made in the milk carton. Slide a second stop onto the skewer, inside the carton.

22. Place the wheel inside the milk carton. Insert the skewer through both of the holes in the middle of the wheel. Slip the third stop onto the skewer.

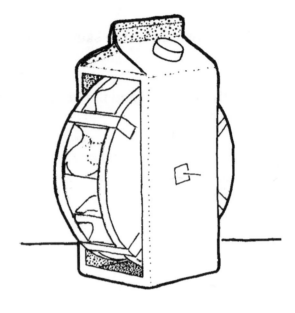

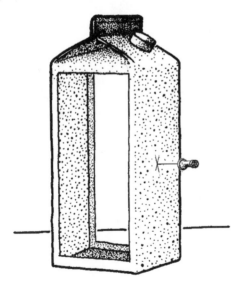

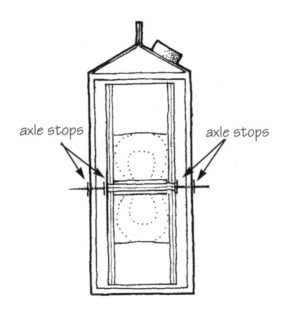

axle stops   axle stops

23. Slide the skewer through the hole on the other side of the carton. Slip the fourth stop onto the skewer, outside the carton.

24. Move the squares on the skewer close to the sides of the carton, so the wheel turns easily but does not wobble.

25. Place the waterwheel under a lightly running hose, under a downspout, or anywhere there's a light flow of water to make the wheel spin around and around!

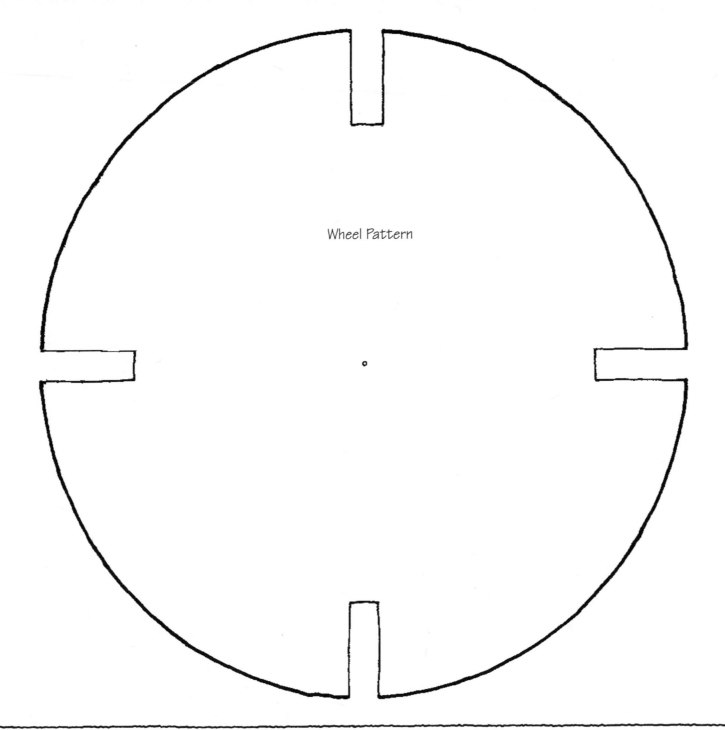

Wheel Pattern

Bubble Makers

*Making bubbles is always fun, and it's even more fun
when you use these bubble makers.*

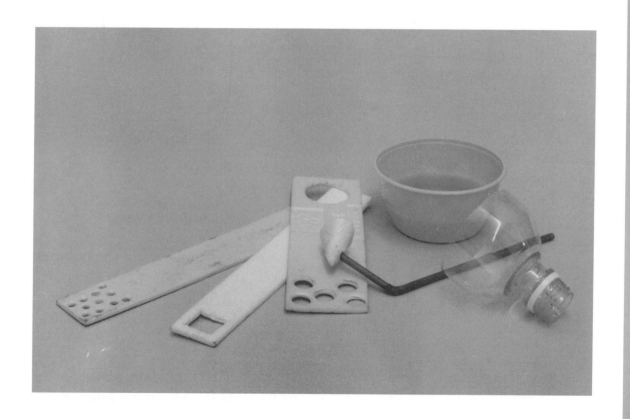

You Need

- ❏ a Styrofoam meat or vegetable tray
- ❏ a small plastic soda bottle
- ❏ a cone-shaped paper cup
- ❏ a flexible plastic straw
- ❏ dishwashing detergent
- ❏ glycerin (You can buy this at a drugstore.)

Have on Hand

- ❏ an eyedropper
- ❏ a large jar with a lid
- ❏ masking tape
- ❏ a measuring cup
- ❏ a spoon
- ❏ water
- ❏ a wide bowl

Tools

- ❏ a pencil
- ❏ a pushpin
- ❏ scissors

Instructions

To Make the Bubble Wand:

1. Wash and dry the Styrofoam tray.

2. Cut off the curved edges of the Styrofoam tray with scissors. Discard the cutoff pieces.

3. Cut one 2½-inch (6.3-cm) -wide strip from the flat Styrofoam tray.

4. Use the ruler and pencil to measure a 1¼-inch (3-cm) square near one end of the strip. Use the Pushpin Method (see page 12) and scissors to cut the square out, as shown.

5. Near the other end of the strip, use the Pushpin Method to cut six or eight holes about ½-inch (1.3-cm) square, as shown.

To Make the Soda-Bottle Blower:

6. Wrap a piece of masking tape around the shoulders of the bottle.

7. Use the Pushpin Method and scissors to cut along the bottom edge of the masking tape.

8. Discard the bottom of the bottle and the bottle cap. Remove the masking tape from the cutoff top portion of the bottle.

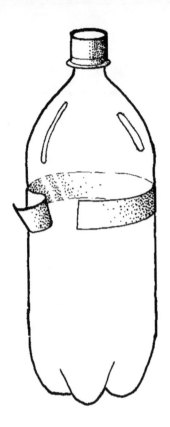

To Make the Bubble Pipe:

9. Use the scissors to cut the pointed tip off the paper cup, about 1½ inches (3.8 cm) up from the point. Save the cutoff tip and discard the larger portion.

10. Make a pushpin hole about ½ inch (1.3 cm) up from the point of the cutoff tip.

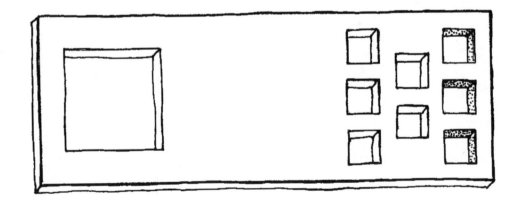

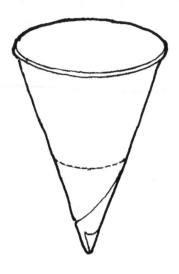

11. Enlarge the pushpin hole with the point of a pencil. The hole should be just large enough to insert the straw snugly.

12. Insert the short end of the straw into the hole you have just made.

To Make the Bubble Mixture:

13. Pour 6 ounces (177 ml) of water into the jar.

14. Pour 2 ounces (60 ml) of dish-washing detergent into the jar.

15. Add five drops of glycerin to the jar with the eyedropper. Glycerin will make the bubbles last longer. If they seem to pop too quickly, add a few more drops.

16. Stir the mixture and pour it into the bowl. If you don't use all the mixture, pour the rest back into the jar and put the lid on the jar.

To Make Bubbles:

17. Dip one end of the Styrofoam wand into the bubble mixture. Scrape off excess bubble mixture onto the edge of the bowl. Blow through the holes or wave the wand in the air.

18. Dip the wide end of the bottle blower in the bubble mixture. You should be able to see a film of bubble liquid across the entire open end. Blow gently through the mouth of the bottle.

19. Pour a very small amount of bubble mixture into the bubble pipe. Blow through the straw to make a froth of small bubbles.

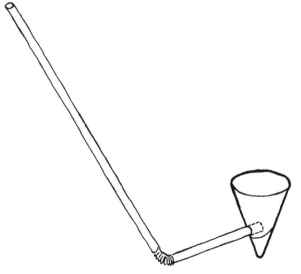

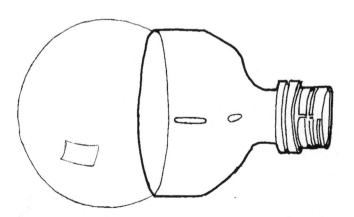

Weather Fun

Barometer

Barometers measure the air pressure, which helps you know what the weather will be like tomorrow. This barometer made from recycled materials will help save the earth and remind you to wear your raincoat!

You Need

- ❏ a 1-quart (946-ml) glass jar, such as a pickle jar
- ❏ a 1-quart (946-ml) glass bottle, such as a vinegar bottle

Note: The neck of the bottle must fit completely into the mouth of the jar. However, there should be a little space between the mouth of the jar and the neck of the bottle. This is easiest if you use a bottle whose neck has ridges around it.

- ❏ adhesive putty (You can buy this at an stationery store.)
- ❏ masking tape

Have on Hand

- ❏ a marking pen
- ❏ paper towels
- ❏ water

Tools

- ❏ a pencil

Instructions

1. For this project, work outdoors or in a sink, where it won't matter if you spill a little water.

2. Remove any labels from the jar and bottle and wash them out thoroughly. Dry the outsides of the jar and bottle completely with paper towels.

3. Fill the jar three-quarters of the way up with water.

4. Fill the bottle three-quarters of the way up with water.

5. Make four small balls of adhesive putty, about the size of a pencil eraser.

6. Make sure that the rim of the jar is completely dry.

7. Stick the balls of putty onto the rim of the jar, evenly spaced.

8. Holding your finger over the mouth of the bottle, turn the bottle upside down and insert it into the mouth of the jar.

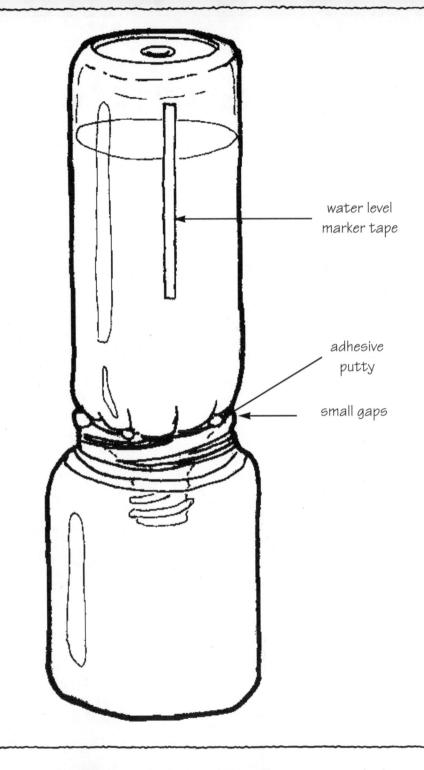

water level marker tape

adhesive putty

small gaps

8. Make sure that the bottle rests on the balls of adhesive putty, and that there is a small gap between the shoulders of the bottle and the rim of the jar. You must have the gap for air to pass through, or the barometer will not work.

9. Use a pencil and ruler to measure a 2-inch (5-cm) piece of tape.

10. Stick the tape to the side of the bottle, centered over the water level.

11. When the water becomes still, use the marking pen to mark the water level on the tape.

12. Place your barometer in a place where it will not be bumped or spilled. Stand the barometer out of the light, where the temperature is cool. A basement or a dark corner would be good.

How the Barometer Works:

13. When it is clear and sunny the air pressure is high. This pushes the water level up. When it is raining and stormy the air pressure is low. This will cause the water level to drop. The change in the water level will be roughly ¼ inch (.6 cm).

14. Often the change in air pressure will occur before the actual change in the weather. Check your barometer in the morning to see if the water level has gone up or down. See if you can predict when the next storm will be.

Recycling Facts & Tips:

Did you know that:

- More than 13 million tons (11.7 million t) of glass are made in the United States each year.

- Glass can be recycled again and again, unlike plastic, which can only be recycled a few times.

How you can help:

- We are already recycling nearly one quarter of the glass containers we use. Every 1-liter glass bottle you recycle saves enough energy to light a light-bulb for 4 hours.

Hygrometer

A thermometer measures how hot it is, but a hygrometer measures how humid it is: how much moisture there is in the air.

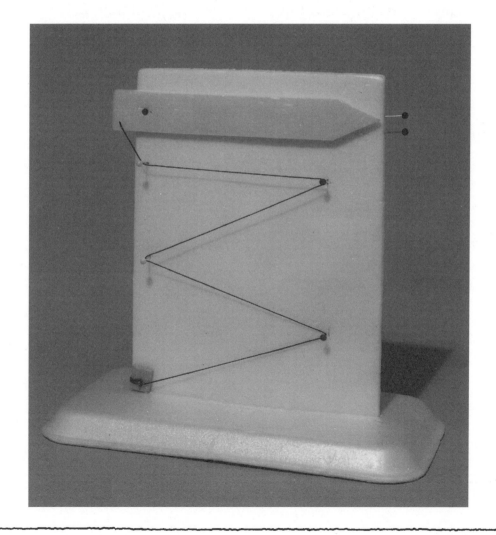

You Need

- ❏ one Styrofoam meat or vegetable tray, 4½ × 8½ inches (11.3 × 21.3 cm)
- ❏ several other large, clean Styrofoam trays
- ❏ seven pins with beaded heads
- ❏ a toothpick
- ❏ black cotton thread, 30 inches (75 cm)

Note: The thread **must** be cotton.

Have on Hand

- ❏ an electric hairdryer
- ❏ a needle
- ❏ a small towel
- ❏ soapy water
- ❏ stick glue

Tools

- ❏ a dull knife (such as a butter knife)
- ❏ a pencil
- ❏ a pushpin
- ❏ scissors

Instructions

1. Wash and dry the Styrofoam trays.

2. Label the 4½ × 8½-inch (11.3 × 21.3-cm) Styrofoam tray A.

3. Cut a ¾ × 8½-inch (1.9 × 15-cm) flat piece of Styrofoam and label it B.

4. Cut a 1½ × 6-inch (3.8 × 15-cm) flat piece of Styrofoam and label it C.

5. Cut a 5½ × 7½-inch (13.8 × 18.8-cm) flat piece of Styrofoam and label it D.

6. Use the Transfer Method (see page 13) to transfer the Base Pattern (page 110) onto piece A.

7. Use the Pushpin Method (see page 12) and the dull knife to cut out the slot you have just marked onto piece A. Cut along the inside of the lines. This piece will be the meter base.

8. Use the scissors to cut one end of piece B into a point. This piece will be the indicator.

9. Measure and draw a grid to divide Piece C into 18 sections that are ½-inch (1.3-cm) square. Cut along the lines you have just drawn.

10. Make five piles of three squares each. Glue each pile together with stick glue. These piles will be pin anchors. Put the three extra squares aside.

11. Transfer the Meter Board Pattern (page 111) onto one side of piece D. This piece will be the meter board.

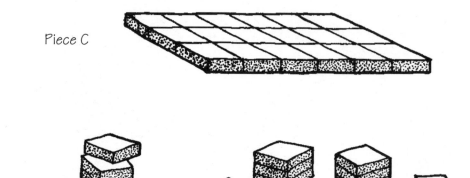

Piece C

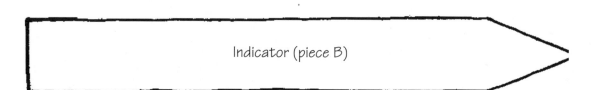

Indicator (piece B)

12. Push one pin through each pin mark on the meter board:

a. For the top pin mark, line up the indicator (piece B) so that its point is lined up with one side of the meter board and it is centered top to bottom over the top pin mark. Push the pin through both the indicator and the meter board.

b. Do not push a pin through the bottom pin mark.

c. Push pins into the side of the meter board as shown on the Meter Board Pattern (page 111). You do not need to do anything more with these two pins until step **14**.

13. Attach the anchors to the back of the meter board:

a. Apply glue to the top of each of the anchors.

b. Press each anchor, glue side in, onto the pins. Press the anchors firmly against the meter board for a few seconds so the glue sets.

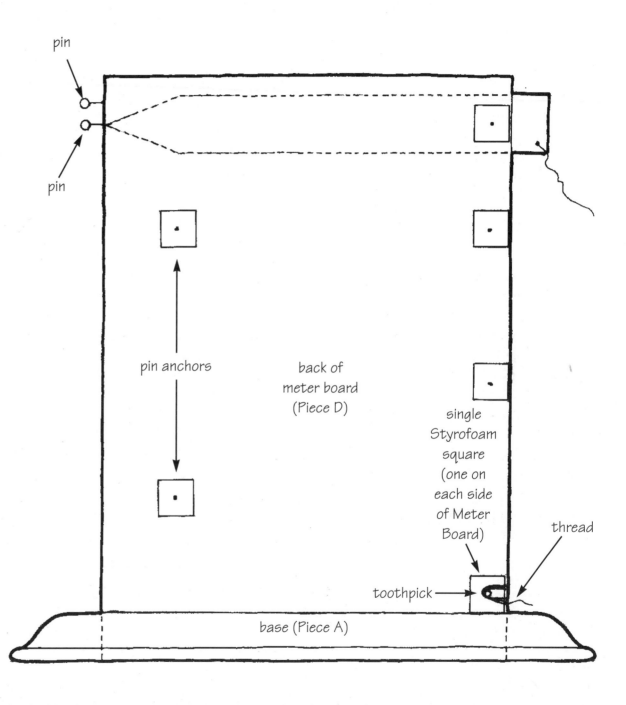

pin

pin

pin anchors

back of meter board (Piece D)

single Styrofoam square (one on each side of Meter Board)

thread

toothpick

base (Piece A)

c. Adjust the pins so that the sharp points don't stick out past the anchors.

14. Glue two of the squares you set aside in step **12** on either side of the bottom pin mark. Wait one hour for the glue to dry before going on to the next step.

15. Break the toothpick in half and push it through the center of the squares covering the bottom pin mark. There should be an equal amount of toothpick sticking out on both sides.

16. Place the meter board into the slot you cut in the base (piece A) in step **4**.

17. You want the point of the indicator to lie between the two pins sticking out from the side of the meter board.

a. Wash the cotton thread with soapy water. Dry it gently with the towel to soak up excess moisture, but make sure it is still damp.

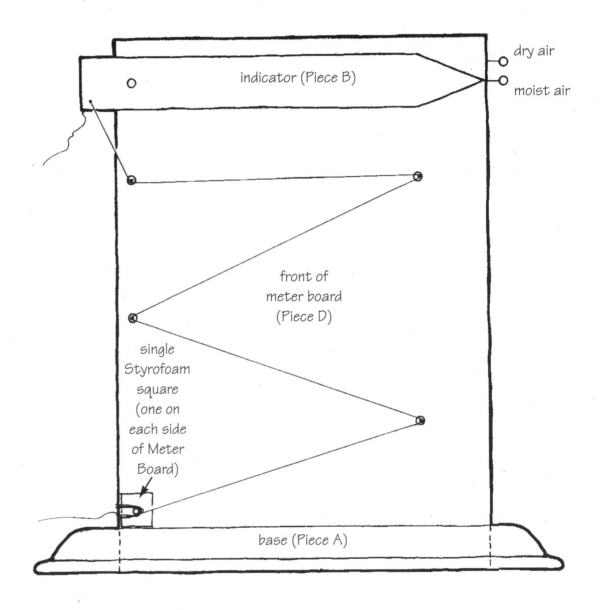

dry air

indicator (Piece B)

moist air

front of meter board (Piece D)

single Styrofoam square (one on each side of Meter Board)

base (Piece A)

b. Thread the needle and tie a large knot near one end of the damp thread.

c. Insert the needle through the back of the indicator, as shown. Pull the thread all the way through so that the knot is lying against the back of the indicator.

d. Trail the thread in a zigzag pattern around the pins, as shown.

e. Pull the thread until the indicator points to the lower pin. Keep it in place by wrapping it around the toothpick, as shown.

Note: If you need to adjust the indicator, move one of the pins on the front of the meter board slightly to the left or right.

18. Testing your Hygrometer:

a. When there is moisture in the air, the thread absorbs as much as it can and gets a little longer. When the air is dry the moisture evaporates and the thread shrinks.

b. To test your hygrometer, use the hair dryer to gently blow hot air onto the damp thread. The indicator will point to the dry pin. Adjust the placement of the dry pin if necessary.

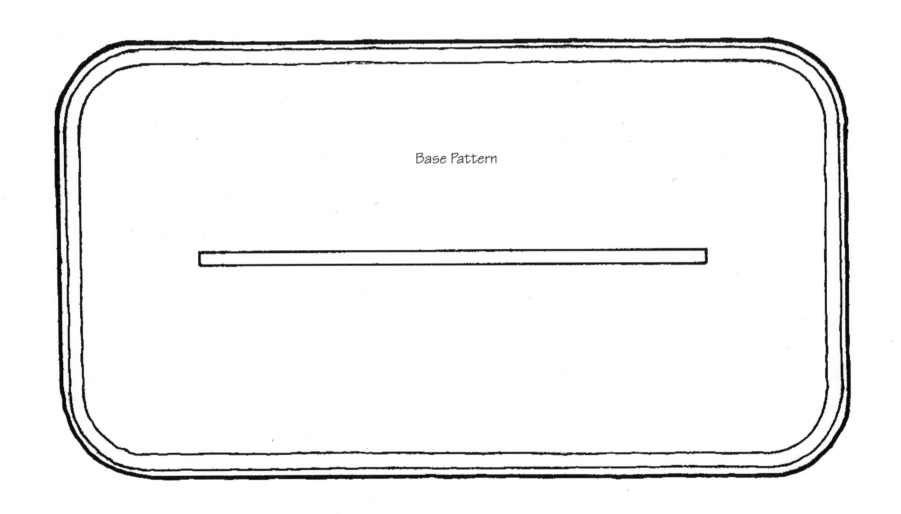

Base Pattern

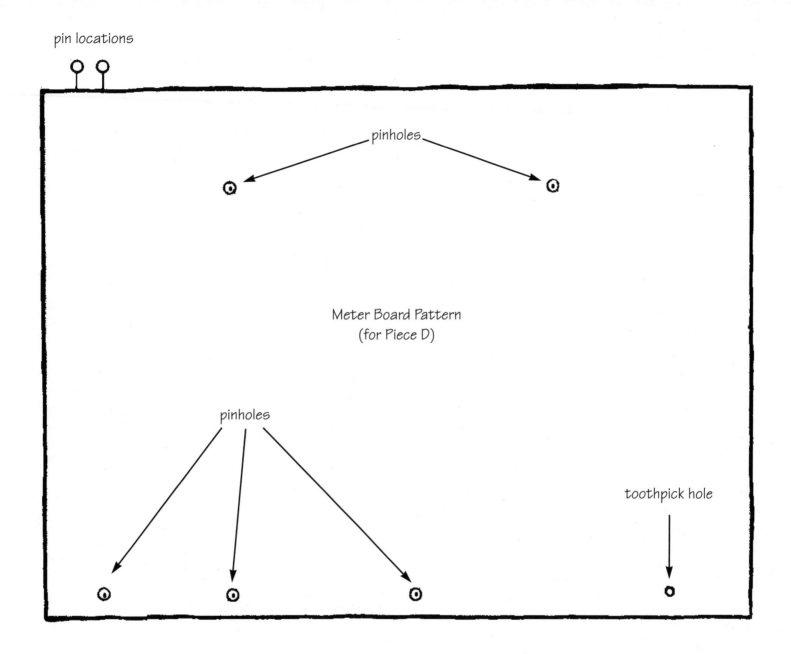

pin locations

pinholes

pinholes

Meter Board Pattern
(for Piece D)

toothpick hole

Rain Gauge

Recycling an old motor oil bottle won't just help reduce the amount of trash we produce, it'll also tell you how much it rained last night!

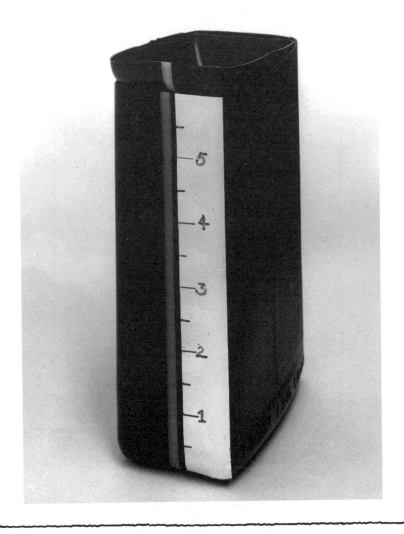

You Need

❏ an empty one-quart (946-ml) plastic motor oil bottle.
Note: Did you know that used motor oil should always be returned to gas stations for safe disposal? It should never be thrown on the ground, as it can pollute the water supply.

Have on Hand

❏ a black permanent marking pen, fine tip
❏ dishwashing liquid
❏ masking tape
❏ newspaper
❏ rags

Tools

❏ a pencil
❏ a pushpin
❏ a ruler
❏ scissors

Instructions

To Clean the Bottle:

1. Remove the cap and prop the bottle upside down on some newspaper. Leave it in this position at least 30 minutes.

2. Squirt some dishwashing liquid into the bottle and fill halfway with water.

3. Replace the cap and shake well.

4. Pour the water out and dry the outside of the bottle with rags. Turn the bottle upside down on the newspaper to drain for 15 minutes.

To Make the Gauge:

5. Use the ruler and pushpin to measure and make two small holes on the sides of the bottle, 6 inches (15 cm) up from the bottom.

6. Wrap a piece of masking tape around the bottle, with its top edge along the pushpin holes, to make a cutting guide, as shown.

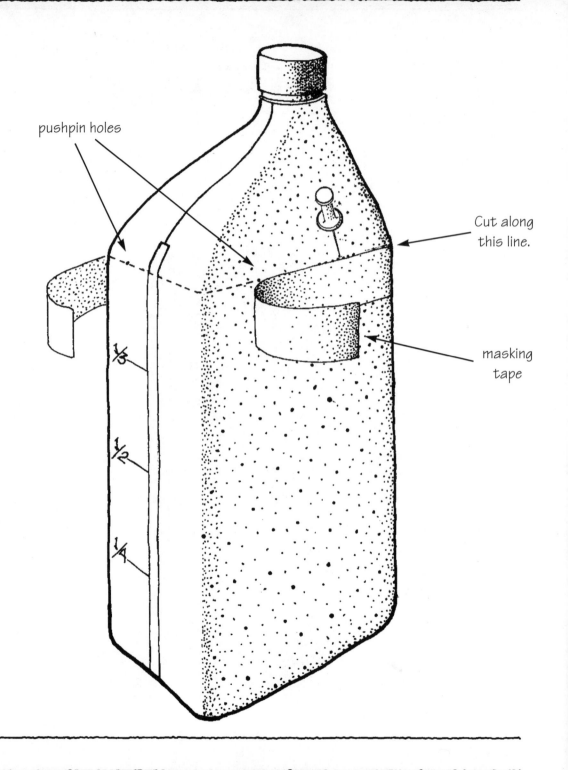

pushpin holes

Cut along this line.

masking tape

1/3

1/2

1/4

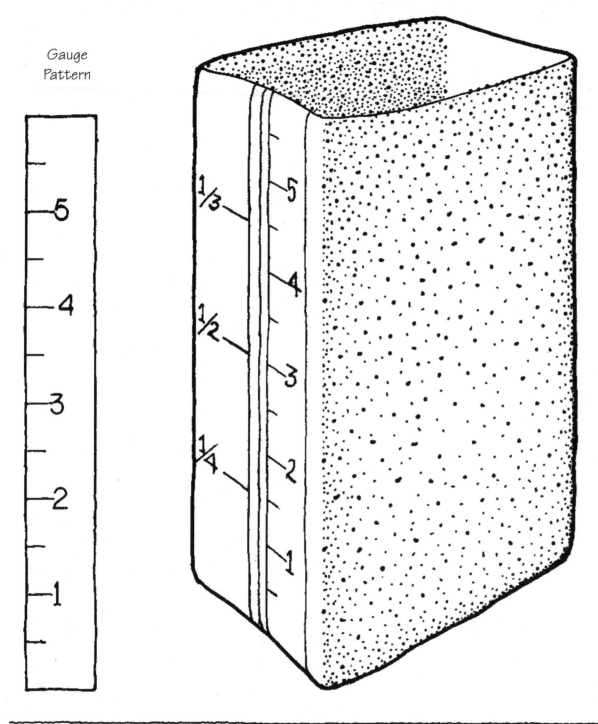

Gauge
Pattern

5

4

3

2

1

1/3

1/2

1/4

5

4

3

2

1

7. Following along the top edge of the tape, use the Pushpin Method (see page 12) and scissors to cut off the top of the bottle. Remove the tape.

8. The inside of the bottle will still be oily. Wipe it with a dry rag and wash it again. Dry it inside and out with a clean rag.

9. Copy the Gauge Pattern onto a 6-inch (15-cm) piece of masking tape. **Note:** The masking tape will have to be replaced occasionally because it is not waterproof.

10. Stick the gauge along the clear strip of plastic on the side of the bottle, as shown.

To Use the Gauge:

11. Place the gauge in an open area outside, away from trees and houses.

12. After it rains, check the gauge and record your readings. Have an adult help you check your measurements against the rainfall recorded in the newspaper. They should be close.

Wind Sock

Want to know which way the wind blows? This decoration made of recyclables will let you know if the wind is blowing, and in which direction.

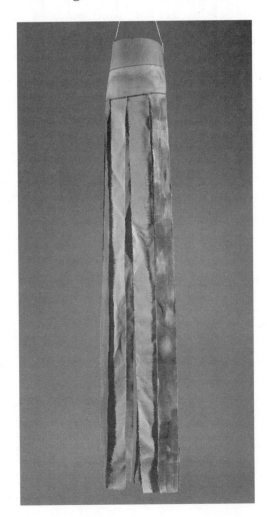

You Need

- ❑ a piece of old, white bed-sheet, 15 × 40 inches (37.5 × 100 cm)
- ❑ a plastic soft-drink bottle, 2-liter size
- ❑ strong string, 14 inches (35 cm) long

Have on Hand

- ❑ a black crayon
- ❑ a black marking pen
- ❑ strapping tape
- ❑ white glue

Tools

- ❑ a pencil
- ❑ a pushpin
- ❑ a ruler
- ❑ scissors

Instructions

1. Use the crayon and ruler to draw the following lines onto the sheet.

a. Draw a line across the sheet 1 inch (2.5 cm) from one end.

b. Draw a second line across the sheet 9 inches (22.5 cm) from the same end.

c. Starting from the opposite end of the sheet, draw four parallel lines from the end of the sheet to the line you drew in **b**. The first line should be 1 inch (2.5 cm) from the right edge of the sheet. The second line should be 3½ inches (8.8 cm) to the left of the first line. The third and fourth lines should each be 3½ inches (8.8 cm) to the left of the previous line.

2. Cut along the lines you have just drawn in **c** to make the streamers.

3. Wash out the plastic bottle carefully.

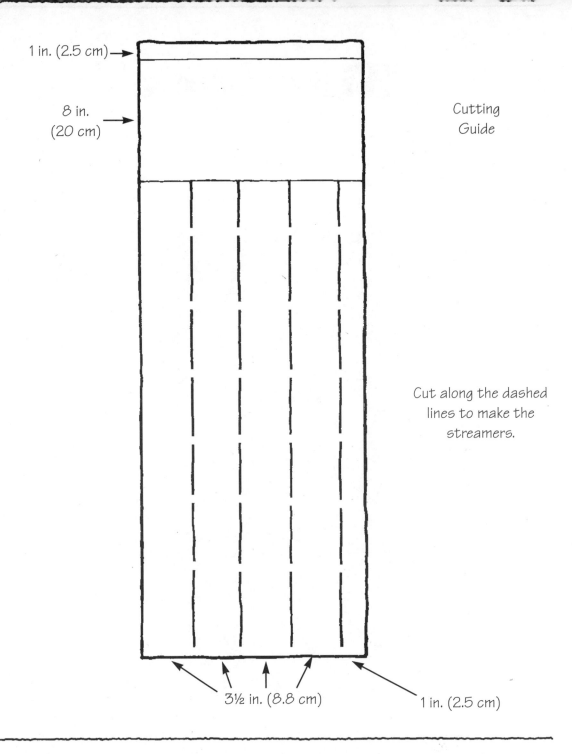

1 in. (2.5 cm)

8 in. (20 cm)

Cutting Guide

Cut along the dashed lines to make the streamers.

3½ in. (8.8 cm)

1 in. (2.5 cm)

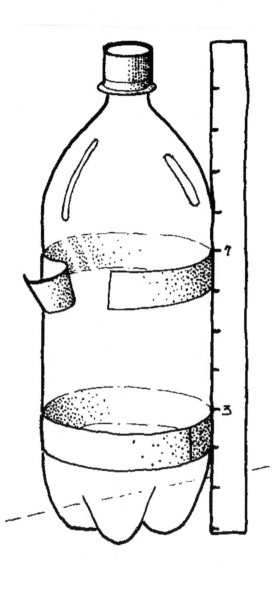

4. Stand the bottle up on a level surface. Hold the ruler on end against the side of the bottle, and make a mark 3 inches (7.5 cm) up from the bottom of the bottle. Repeat in several places around the bottle.

5. Repeat step **4**, this time making marks 7 inches (17.5 cm) up from the bottom of the bottle.

6. Wrap a piece of masking tape around the bottle, lining up the top edge of the tape with the upper marks you have just drawn.

7. Wrap a second piece of masking tape around the bottle, lining up the top edge of the tape with the lower marks.

8. Use the Pushpin Method (see page 12) and scissors to cut along the top edges of the two strips of tape. Recycle the top and bottom of the bottle. You should be left with a 4-inch (10-cm) plastic cylinder. This will be the collar.

9. Use short strips of strapping tape to attach 1 inch (2.5 cm) of the solid end of the fabric you cut in steps **1** and **2** to the outside of the plastic collar.

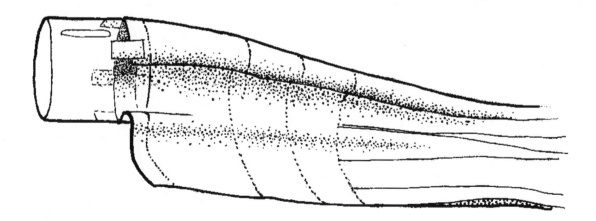

10. Gently push the remainder of the fabric through the collar, as shown.

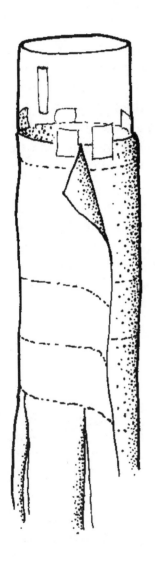

11. Pull the fabric over the outside of the collar, so that the entire collar is covered with fabric. Adjust the fabric so the streamers hang loosely off the collar.

12. Place dots of white glue under the top layer of fabric near the bottom edge of the collar, where the streamers start. Press each spot down firmly so the glue can set.

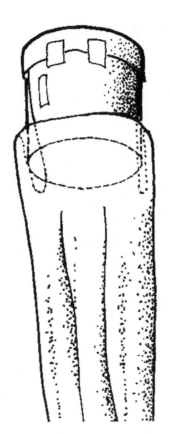

13. Use a pencil and ruler to mark a spot ¾ inch (1.9 cm) from the top edge of the collar (opposite from where the streamers are). Make another mark exactly opposite it on the other side of the collar. Use the pushpin to make holes where you made the marks.

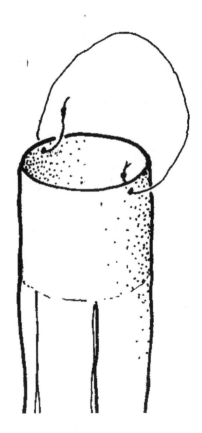

14. Enlarge the holes so they are large enough to pass the string through.

15. Pass one end of the string through each hole from the outside so the string forms a handle. Make a large knot at each end so the string cannot slip out.

16. Hang your wind sock by its string to a low branch.

17. Watching the wind sock blow in the wind will tell you both what direction the wind is blowing and how hard it is blowing.

✪ **Even Better:** Decorate your wind sock with crayons, markers, or watercolor paints.

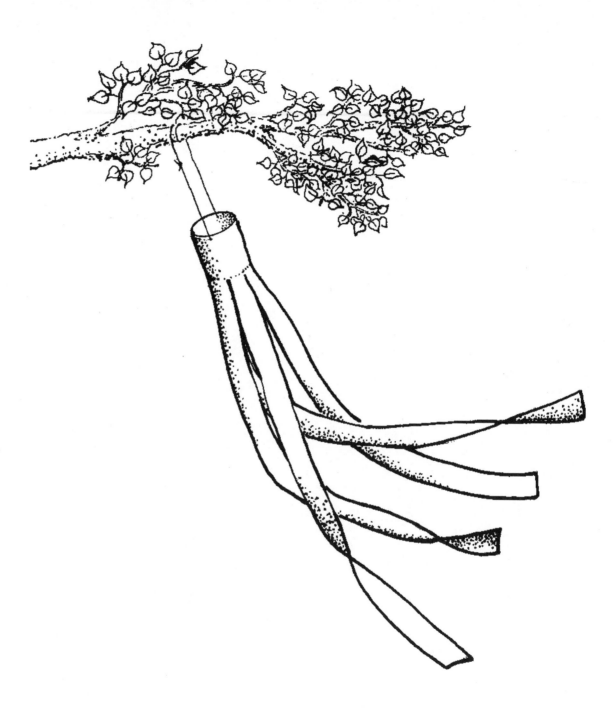

Weather Log

Use this log to keep track of the readings from the other weather instruments you have made in this chapter.

You Need

❏ a used file folder
❏ outdoor scenes cut from magazines

Have on Hand

❏ stick glue

Tools

❏ a pencil
❏ scissors

Instructions

To Make the Weather Log:

1. Use the stick glue to cover the outside of the file folder with outdoor scenes cut from magazines.

trim

trim

2. Use the scissors to trim off any pieces of magazine pictures that are hanging over the edges of the cardboard.

3. Use a photocopier to make several copies of the Weather Log on page 125, or draw your own log on scrap paper.

4. Place the pages of your weather log inside the decorated folder.

5. Your Weather Log is ready to use.

To Use the Weather Log:

6. In the appropriate spaces, record your weather readings.

7. Record whether your barometer is higher or lower than the original mark. If you like, you can make a pencil mark each day and record the change from the previous day's reading as well. Record your readings as Steady High, Steady Low, Moving High or Moving Low.

8. Record whether your hygrometer says that the air is Moist, Dry, or In Between.

9. Record how much rain, if any, has fallen into your rain gauge. If it only rained a little, record "less than 1 inch (2.5 cm)."

10. Record in which direction the wind is blowing. If you aren't sure, ask an **adult** to help you find out which way north, south, east, and west are. Also, estimate the wind speed as None, Some, Strong, or Very Strong.

11. Look at the clouds in the sky. Record your observations of the cloud cover as Clear, Partly Cloudy, or Overcast.

12. You might also look at an outdoor thermometer to record the temperature.

13. Guess what kind of weather you think will come later today and tomorrow. Record your predictions, and check back to see if you were right. If you need to, read the directions for the weather projects again to see how they can help you understand and predict the weather.